BUILD A
PROPERTY TAX APPEAL:
HOW TO ADJUST FOR
DIFFERENCES & FINALIZE
TRUE MARKET VALUE

Put Facts and Figures Together!

George Evers

About The Author

George Evers served in the U.S. Marine Corps and spent considerable time in the construction trades. He is a university graduate, entrepreneur, construction expert, appraiser, property tax consultant, marketer, investor, author, publisher from Lake Hopatcong, New Jersey.

He has created and sold more than $100,000,000 in merchandise, information and other transactions and services over his career.

George is an author of 3 books, as well as a property tax consulting business course found at http://propertytaxconsult.com

Limits of Liability/Disclaimer

This publication is designed to provide accurate, authoritative and current information. The publisher is not engaged in rendering legal or other professional service and the ideas, suggestions, general principles and conclusions presented in this text may be subject to local, state and federal laws and regulations, court cases and any revisions of the same.

The author and publisher of this book and the accompanying materials have used his best effort in preparing this program. The author and publisher makes no representation or warranties with respect to the accuracy, applicability, fitness or completeness of the contents of this program.

He disclaims any warranties (expressed or implied), merchantability, or fitness for any particular purpose. The

Review Page

Please review my book on Amazon.com,

Thank You.

Table of Contents

8

CHAPTER 1: OVERVIEW AND METHOD OF PROPERTY TAX REDUCTION

"Diverse weights and diverse measurements are both an abomination to the Lord." - Proverbs 20:10

INTRODUCTION

Welcome to the world of appraising the value of houses! With this book you can clearly and accurately determine the market value of your home or any other home, for that matter. You will also be able to determine if your property tax assessment is out of line and, if so, how to champion a successful tax appeal.

Are your property taxes too high? Do you want to do something about it? The process of reducing your property taxes can be frustrating and confusing and can leave you wondering if you are correctly approaching the task to maximize the chances of winning your appeal. The aim of this book is to demystify the appeal process, help optimize the time spent on preparing your appeal and, ultimately, help you win your appeal.

We'll show you what specific information to gather, where to get this information, how to prepare an appeal and what to adjust for in valuing your property. We will suggest to you what to say and what not to say to the taxing authority before whom you are appealing. We have also provided sample forms that you can access online for you to photocopy and use in preparing and presenting your appeal.

HOW YOUR TAX RATE IS DETERMINED

You don't need a detailed understanding of the whole process, but grasping a few facts will help. First, it is necessary for the taxing authority to know the amount of money (the budget) the local government will spend for one year. The local government provides income for regulatory and service departments, schools, police and fire departments, road maintenance, library, etc.

The total budget is composed of these salaries and expenses along with bonded indebtedness (principal and interest payments on borrowed money that was voted for). This budget is then divided by the total dollar amount of all the assessed value of real estate in the tax district (provided by the assessor) to determine your tax rate.

That tax rate when multiplied by your property value (assessed value determined by the tax assessor) equals your tax bill. For additional details, see Chapter 6 under the section, The Mass Appraisal Process and Yearly Revaluation Districts.

More detailed information on the tax rate follows. **Do not worry if you do not completely understand it, as it is not essential in ascertaining the facts for your case.** The tax rate may be expressed as mills or as a percentage.

It may be shown as dollars per hundred ($7.00 per hundred, shown as .07) and may also be known as the mill rate (millage means per thousand). For example, a millage rate quoted as 70 mills would be equivalent to a tax rate of $70.00 per thousand in valuation.

Varying assessment ratios and tax rates can have the same tax effect on a property. In the following example, the mill rate is the number of mills per dollar of assessed value; the assessment is expressed as a percentage of market value.

Market Value	$80,000
Assessment Ratio	90% (.90 x $80,000 = $72,000)
Assessment	$72,000
Tax Rate	50 mills
Taxes	$3,600 (.050 x $72,000)

Another tax district or even a community within the same tax district may be assessed at 55% (sales ratio) but with a higher tax rate of 82 mills yet resulting in nearly equal taxes.

Market Value	$80,000
Assessment Ratio	55% (.55 x $80,000 = $44,000)
Assessment	$44,000
Tax Rate	82 mills
Taxes	$3,608 (.082 x $44,000)

Some states express taxes in dollars per hundred. The same $80,000 property, with a similar assessment and paying the same amount of tax might appear as:

Market Value	$80,000
Assessment Ratio	55%
Assessment	$44,000
Tax Rate	$8.20 per hundred (for dollar amount move decimal left two places)
Taxes	**$3,608 (.082 x $44,000)**

FACTORS THAT RESULT IN PROPERTY TAX REDUCTION

Criteria that may bring about a property tax reduction include:

1. **Taxability** - which refers to exempt status and is rarely the case (see page 94).

2. **Mechanical Errors** - refers to computational errors, incorrect property sketches and measurements of the floor plan of your residence.

3. **Fair Market Value** - concerns property that is appraised at a value higher than the most probable price it would bring in a sale occurring under normal market conditions.

The most common tax reduction given a property owner is due to a re-assessment based on fair market value (#3 above). Since, by all likelihood, you'll use the fair market value approach in your appeal, this area will be our primary focus and will be covered in detail in Chapter 3.

Mechanical errors are discussed in Chapter 6 under the section: Property Record Cards. Taxability is also discussed in Chapter 6 under the section: Tax Exemptions.

DO YOU HAVE A CASE?

First, we have to determine if you have a case at all, that is, if your assessments are too high. The amount of your assessment is what the town thinks your house and property are worth relative to other properties. This may or may not be an accurate figure.

The National Taxpayers Union is credited as saying that as much as 50% of all property in America is over assessed. Recently appraised properties are more accurate and closer to the dollar amount of current value than properties that have not been appraised recently. In other words, a recent estimate is closer to reality than an old estimate.

Many taxpayers have the impression that their assessment is fair if it is below the current fair market value. However, what we really are looking for is equitability. The fact is that property should be valued equitably with similar type property within the same taxing jurisdiction. If a taxpayer's property is assessed at 95% of fair market value and, in the rest of the jurisdiction, similar properties are assessed at 75% of fair market value, what's fair about that?

The question is, what does the taxing authority think your house is worth? After you have determined this figure, you will be armed with a number to compare to other similar properties and determine if you are over assessed.

To determine this figure, call the municipal taxing authority where you live and request the tax assessor's office. Ask for the **sales ratio.** This can be called, depending on the jurisdiction, the average ratio, assessment level, director's ratio, the common level of 100% of true value, RAR (residential assessment ratio) or the equalization rate (which may not always be equivalent to the sales ratio).

Ask for the current assessed valuation for your land as well as the amount of assessment for improvements (your house) and the total value for both. Obtain the legal description of your land known as the lot and block number or parcel identification number (PIN number).

This information should also be on your tax bill. Calculate the total assessed value of your house and property (add them) and divide the total assessed value of your residence by the sales ratio to determine what your tax appraiser thinks your house and property are worth.

For example:

$25,000 land + $193,000 improvements (residence) $218,000 total assessed valuation

If the sales ratio for the year was 71.7% then your home is valued at $304,044.63

NOTE:

This is what the taxing authority thinks your property and residence are worth but **not** necessarily what it will sell for in the open residential housing market.

Total Assessed Valuation divided by sales ratio = <u>what they think your land</u> <u>and dwelling(s) are worth</u> but **not** always what it will sell for in the marketplace.

> (mathematical note: remember that when using your sales ratio percentage figure as a divisor, move the decimal point 2 spaces to the left.)

Now you are armed with what the taxing authority **thinks** your residence is worth. You can now compare this figure to the actual amount your property and house would get in the open marketplace. If this figure is <u>more</u> than the fair open market value for your house, you are over assessed and chances are favorable that you have a case.

At this juncture you may have only a ball park notion of what your house is worth. If that figure is out of line with the assessor's figure, you should proceed with a residential market analysis of your property's actual worth.

To Recap:

Assessed Value divided by Sales Price = **Sales Ratio**

Sales Ratio multiplies by Sales Price = **Assessed Value**

Assessed Value divided by Sales Ratio = **Sales Price (Market Value)**

Your assessments should be broken down into two components: land value and house (improvement) value.

Adjustments are made to either the current assessed land value or to the current assessed improved value.

For instance, if the subject property is located next to a major noisy highway and the comps are not, a major deduction would be made and assigned to the property component for the assessment.

If your house has a deteriorated roof that needs replacement and the comps used have newer roofs, an adjustment would be made to the current assessed improved value for the subject property to reflect that negative condition.

Parcel Value Example

Item	Current Assessed Value	FY 2013 Assessed Value
Buildings	84,280	37,940
Extra Bldg Features	0	0
Outbuildings	0	0
Land	90,370	39,060
Total:	**174,650**	**77,000**

For this year, they are saying that 48% of your total assessments are for improvements (buildings) and 52% are for land.

Land portion to total property ratio = .52
Property portion to total property ratio = .48
$84,280 / .70 = $120,400= **what they think your structure is worth**
$90,379 / .70 = $129,100= **what they think your land is worth**

$84,280 and $90,370 represent 70% of what the city thinks the building and the land are worth (its market value) therefore you must divide by .70.

The city thinks that the combined worth or market value of the property is $249,500.

To contest the assessment, you'll need to find comparables that, after you do the valuation adjustments, arrive at a lower finalized total value than your subject home (or whatever arbitrary percentage discrepancy the town allows for a challenge to initiate) in order to win your case.

METHODS OF COMPARISON

There are 3 common methods to find the value of a property:

1. Cost approach.

2. Income approach.

3. Fair market value comparison approach.

The best and most widely-used approach to use in your tax appeal is the **fair market value comparison approach.** This approach uses sales and appraisal data and examines the current relationship between these two factors.

This is done by comparing the market value of your house to other houses of similar size, location, etc. which have recently been sold.

1. The cost approach is used by the assessor to value your property. Because it values each component of a building structurally, it is difficult to use.

2. The <u>income approach</u> is used when valuing income-producing property. Even though residential property is sometimes rented, the income approach is generally not used.

3. The <u>fair market value comparison approach</u> uses the principle of substitution. The principle of substitution states that the maximum value of your house and property tends to be set by the sales price of an equivalent, equally desirable, similar substitute house and property, for a certain date in time.

This market approach is most easily understood and most relied upon by the taxing authorities to capture the realistic value of your house and property. There are four basic phases involved in this approach:

- Recording and analyzing data from your property and potential comparable properties
- Selecting the appropriate comparable data
- Developing reasonable adjustments based on market data
- Applying your findings to the subject (your property)

The fair market value comparison approach is fully covered in Chapter 3 and is expressed as the following formula:

Sales Price of Comparable Property + or - Adjustments = Market Value of Subject Property (your property)

THE NEXT STEP: VISITING THE TAX OFFICE

If it appears you have a case, visit your municipal and/or county taxing authorities and ask for their printed instructions and appeal forms. These are usually brief. Be certain to obtain answers to the following questions:

- Annual assessment date (common date that all appeal evidence must precede).
- Annual filing date (deadline date by which appeal must be filed).
- Amount of filing fee.
- PIN number(s) (parcel identification number) or lot and block number(s).
- Current assessments for your land and improvements.
- Current sales ratio for that year.
- Is there a minimum or maximum common level range.
- Copy of property record card.
- Exemptions that are recognized in your state.

SALES RATIO

Every year the taxing authority releases a different figure for their sales ratio. As stated previously, it can be called the average ratio, assessment level, the common level of 100% true value, average percentage of full value, current ratio, the equalization rate (which may not always be equivalent to the sales ratio), the director's ratio, just valuation, the RAR (residential assessment ratio), and there may be other names or names in the making.

The main point is to be sure to use the current sales ratio for the tax year against which you are appealing. Every year has its own particular corresponding ratio.

California's Proposition 13

California passed a law called Proposition 13. Proposition 13 helps by limiting the maximum tax rate to 1%. If a home has the value of $500,000, the owner will see a tax bill of $5,000. Furthermore, the tax rate can only go up 2% a year. In other states, if the value of the home doubles, so does the tax rate.

Since there is no sales ratio in the bill, local governments can levy no more property taxes than levied the previous year, with the exception of new construction, without a vote of the electorate. The rub is, are the property values calculated right in the first place?

Consumer Reports says that 40% of property tax assessments are in error. Besides, homes deteriorate, situations change, comparables change, neighborhoods change and valuations change. There still remains a need to determine if the underlying assessment by the tax assessor for a home's market value is realistic or NOT.

ANNUAL ASSESSMENT DATE

The taxing authority designates a common date called the "annual assessment date" and it precedes your annual deadline filing date. The sale dates of the comparable properties you choose must precede this assessment date. If the annual assessment date is in October and your appeal is scheduled for August, you must have sales comparables dating before the October assessment date of the preceding year to be valid, otherwise your evidence will not be accepted.

For example, if your appeal was scheduled for August 10, 2013 and your annual assessment date is October 1, 2012, get comparable sales dated before October 1, 2012. Another example: if your annual assessment date is December 31, 2012 and your appeal is scheduled for February of 2013, the facts and evidence must be gathered from comparables sold before December 31, 2012.

HUNTING FOR COMPARABLES

Finding houses similar to yours that sold at or before the required assessment date is most easily accomplished by visiting your local real estate office and browsing through expired multiple listing books.

You must find 3 comparable properties most similar to and in the vicinity of your property. Most real estate offices are friendly, looking to build good public relations and will generally be receptive to your plight. You may be a source of future business to them and help them gain a listing with a favorable recommendation.

"Visits should be like a winter's day; lest you're too troublesome hasten away" - Benjamin Franklin

The real estate agent will guide you to the appropriate information in the Multiple Listing Service (MLS) "Sold" books. The MLS books will contain photographs of the property that sold and detailed descriptive data about the sold listing.

You have to look in the *sold section* of the expired listings to find listings similar to yours. Pay special attention to properties with similar number of rooms, number of bedrooms and baths to yours and share a similar neighborhood or are in the vicinity of the one in which you live.

23

The more closely the comparables resemble the subject property (your property), the more credible your basis for an adjusted valuation will be. If, for instance, you live in a lake front home, find other lake front houses with which to compare. Try to find as many recently sold, similar designed homes comparable to yours as you can. Don't compare a 1-story ranch to a 2-story colonial. If possible, compare ranches to ranches, bi-levels to bi-levels, colonials to colonials.

After you have found the information you need, ask to photocopy these three properties for further reference. Also, photocopy many extra similar properties for further reference because, as you scrutinize your information, you may find something previously overlooked and may possibly need to find another comparable more similar to your property.

Another great source of information is the "open house." Real estate agencies will host an open house to better expose the homes they have contracted to sell. Usually, they will have a data sheet for attendees giving a description of the house and property, a survey and a list of the home's selling features. You can scrutinize features similar to or different from your home and when the house sells, you can use it as a comparable.

Concentrate on finding comparable sales that have characteristics similar to those of your own home. A variety of these parameters are listed below in descending rank of importance, the first listed being more important than the last listed.

Categories of Compatibility

- Similar neighborhood
- Total square feet of living space
- Number of rooms, bedrooms, baths

- Sold within 12 months prior to the annual assessment date, preferably within 4 months of it
- Sales price within general market price of subject
- Sales or financing concessions
- Location
- Quality of construction
- Style house
- Age of house
- Condition
- Sq. ft. property site and view
- Functional utility
- Number of garages
- Swimming pool, fireplace(s), remodeled kitchen, kitchen equipment, etc.
- Storm windows or replacement windows or thermopane windows
- Basement i.e. finished, unfinished or none
- Deck, patio, porch, etc.
- Landscaping that's similar

CHAPTER 2: THE ADJUSTMENT PROCESS

"...skilled tracking is a mark of a great hunter and a great warrior." - Louis L'Amour in *Jubal Sacket*

PROBABLE PRICE

An appraisal is an opinion of value, an estimate of worth. The Federal National Mortgage Association (FNMA) states, "Market value is the most *probable price* which a property should bring in a competitive and open market under all conditions requisite to a fair sale, the buyer and seller, each acting prudently, knowledgeable and assuming the price is not affected by undue stimulus." [1] The value of residential real estate is estimated by comparing the subject with <u>similar properties</u> that have been sold recently. Look at your neighborhood to find comparable sales or properties in similar neighborhoods that share similar characteristics of lifestyles, income level of residents, surroundings, average age and value of houses.

Neighborhoods have boundaries and barriers to the next neighborhood which may signal an abrupt change in life-style i.e. railroad tracks, freeways, highways, major traffic arteries, lakes, rivers, mountains, etc. There are political boundaries created for government purposes, such as school districts, assessment districts, zoning districts and city limits. In your neighborhood analysis, you may consider recreational facilities common to your situation. The focus is to find comparable homes in similar neighborhoods for your analysis.

ADJUSTMENTS

Because properties are seldom alike, it will be necessary to make adjustments between the comparable properties as compared to the subject property (your property). This process equalizes the properties in the comparison. An adjustment is "a decrease or increase in the sales price of a comparable property to account for a feature that the property has or does not have in comparison to the subject property." (2)

In other words, the comparable properties are adjusted to reflect the value of the subject property. You never adjust the subject (your own home). If two houses were identical in every way except that the subject (your house) had a deck and the comparable did not, the value of the comparable would be adjusted upward.

Take time to browse market analysis pages in order to gain familiarity with the sample market analysis layout. By this method, the subject (your house) reflects more value when compared to a comparable house with deficient items (such as no deck or no garage). Always remember: <u>comparable sales must be adjusted and not the subject property</u>. "The subject property is the standard against which the comparable sales are evaluated and adjusted.

Thus, if an item in the comparable property is superior to that in the subject property, a minus (-) adjustment is required to make that item equal to that in the subject property. Conversely, if an item in the comparable property is inferior to that in the subject property, a plus (+) adjustment is required to make that item equal to that in the subject property." (3)

In other words, if a comparable sale property has a major improvement that your property does not have, make a

27

minus adjustment. On the other hand, if you enjoy a major improvement and the comparative sale property does not, make a positive adjustment.

Round off adjustments to the nearest $100. Your adjustments are based on market data and supported by market evidence.[4]

LIMITS FOR ADJUSTMENTS

Gross adjustments, that is, the total individual adjustments measuring differences in any given comparable to your house and lot, should be no greater than **25%** of the sales price. Any net adjustment, that is, any individual adjustment reflecting a difference between the comparable and your house and lot, should be no greater than **15%** of the sales price. [5] Remember, the more the comparables are like your house, the less adjustments will be necessary and the more accurate the appraisal will be. To avoid scrutiny, it is best that individual adjustments not be above 10%. Large adjustments indicate incomparable sales. If a large adjustment is necessary, an addendum narrative with explanations and evidence should be included.

Examples of some typical adjustment figures for dissimilarities between a subject property and its comparables, are given throughout this book for houses of average quality. Nevertheless, you must determine what is realistic for your particular property and appropriate for your area.

TWO METHODS FOR DETERMINING VALUE FOR ANY FEATURE

Matched Pair Extraction: In theory, adjustments using a market approach for a particular item are best supported by looking at a matched pair of sales. For example, if you are looking to establish the value of a one-car garage, find a recently sold house that is exactly the same in every aspect except lacking the particular item (in this case a one-car garage) for which value is trying to be established.

Sometimes a matched pair analysis may involve making multiple adjustments for several differences in order to define a specific item's value. However, fewer adjustments equal greater accuracy. It is usually difficult, if not impossible, to find pure and equivalent supporting sales data. Few, if any, appraisers attempt to find value by this method.

Cost Survey Method: "Reproduction cost new (what it cost to replace an item), less depreciation from all (subsequent) causes equals value."[6] Different components of a house depreciate at different rates, i.e. roof shingles may last 20 years, inside paint 8 years, an air conditioner 15 years.

One federal loan agency's instructions read, "When the number of comparable sales is limited in the market area, an appraiser may be unable to complete a matched pair extraction for value differences. In such cases, *cost data* for items such as air conditioning, storage, fireplace, etc., may be used. Cost survey results may be used to estimate value differences for features such as location, site/view, design and appeal, etc. because of the appraiser's inability to objectively measure value for these type features."[7]

Cost data survey information can be obtained from Marshall & Swift Residential Cost Handbook or other cost estimating manuals. Look under Appendix C for other cost estimation sources. Depreciation is discussed more in the Depreciation Chapter.

INFORMATION SOURCES

For further information and for authentic dollar amounts to use in adjusting for a particular item when determining a <u>cost approach</u> to value, Marshall and Swift Residential Cost Handbook provides an excellent reference. You can find it in most larger libraries. Marshall and Swift contains individual building costs for various style buildings for all 50 states, the U.S Territories and the Canadian Provinces.

Cost rate multipliers are listed for every geographical territory. Other popular cost manuals are Means Cost Calculator, Boeckh Building Manual, and Dodge Building Manual found in your local or county library (the county library is the most likely source). See Appendix B for a complete description of likely sources of information.

Another fast and expedient way to get a <u>market value</u> figure for a particular item or structure is to speak to the local tax assessor, appraiser or loan officer at a financial institution where you do business. Ask for a figure to check against for a particular adjustment you have in mind.

Most people in the profession are very co-operative as long as you don't waste too much of their time. Bring a picture of the item you are seeking to evaluate. Attach it to a blank sheet of paper and get it signed and dated to further validate the value for a particular item. Include this in your appeal as supplemental evidence if it is accurate and supports your appeal. Appraisal firms often make disrupting phone calls to individuals to find financial data in their search for market value. Appraisal firms should be willing to reciprocate and answer a question or two if you keep the call courteous and brief.

The Comparative Market Analysis (CMA) that real estate brokers employ is not a bona fide appraisal. Real estate firms may provide this for free or for a small charge. It is not thorough, complete, supportable or defensible in most situations. Do not use this information in a tax appeal. However, for valuation on specific items, a Realtors® professional designation is respected as an authority on market conditions and his or her opinion has some auxiliary value.

NATIONAL SURVEY RESULTS OF REAL ESTATE AND APPRAISAL PROFESSIONALS

COSTS VS. VALUE OF IMPROVEMENT: Survey of Realtors®

Each year, hundreds of real-estate agents nationwide are asked to rate improvements. *Remodeling* magazine, a trade publication for contractors, publishes a yearly financial pay back survey and compiles it in its annual *Cost vs. Value Report*. This 2006 report [8] identifies and ranks building projects that deliver the best return for money spent on them. **2006 Cost vs. Value Report From Remodeling Magazine**:

http://www.remodeling.hw.net/

The national average percentage return and average total cost of each building project follow:

> **98.5% Minor Kitchen Remodel:** Update a 200 sq. ft. kitchen. Refinish 30 lineal feet of cabinetry with new raised panel wood doors, install new countertops, wall covering, resilient flooring, new oven and cooking surface. Repaint. Average cost: $14,913

86.4% Second Bathroom: Add a second bath to a one or a one-and-a-half-bath home within existing floor plan. Add a 6 x 8-foot bathroom with bathtub, sink, medicine cabinet, linen storage cabinet, new lighting, ceramic tile on floor and in tub area. Average cost: $22,977. (A conservative cost range for money spent on this type of improvement should not exceed 10%-15% of house value.)

83% Family-Room Addition: Add 16-by-25-foot to existing home, crawl space foundation, 180 sq. ft. of glazing (doors, windows, 2 skylights), hardwood floors, tie in electric, heating and cooling. Average cost: $54,773

93.5% Converting Unfinished Attic into Extra Bedroom and Bath: Convert attic to a 15 by 15-ft. bedroom and 5-by-7-ft. shower bath, install 4 windows, 15-ft. shed dormer, closet under eves, insulation, carpet, tie in heat, cooling and electric. Average cost: $39,188.

102.2% Remodeled Bath: Update existing 5-by-7-foot, 25+ year old bathroom with new fixtures, double sink, recessed vanity, new lighting, ceramic wall tile and flooring, wallpaper. Average cost : $10,499.

95.5% Siding Replacement: Replace 1,250 sq. ft. of existing siding with new vinyl siding, including trim. Average cost: $7,239.

90.3% Deck Addition: Add a 16-by-20-foot deck of pressure treated pine, including built-in bench, railings and planter. Average cost: $11,294.

89.6% Window Replacement: Replace 10 existing 3-by-5-foot windows with aluminum-clad or vinyl windows, including new trim. Not to disturb inside trim. Average cost $9,684.

VARIOUS UPGRADES: COST VS PAY BACK[9]

100%-1,000% cosmetic improvements New carpets, fresh paint, upgraded lighting fixtures, repairing broken windows, landscaping touch-ups, etc.

80%-100% bath skylight Doubles as a "greenhouse" with humidity supplied by the shower.

77%-97% wood windows Vinyl windows or aluminum windows do not pay back the same as interior revealing wood windows.

65%-80% deck Constructed with pressure-treated pine material. Cedar decks appear richer and are more splinter resistant offering still higher pay backs.

30%-50% top brand-name appliances Standard size commonly used appliances.

30%-40% basement conversion Buyers look at basements as a do-it-yourself project.

30%-35% energy upgrades Buyers are reluctant to pay the full cost of professionally installed thermal windows.

0%- 85% swimming pool However appealing, buyers do not like maintenance responsibility and insurance costs.

For what single feature are all buyers most looking? The National Association of Home Builders reported in a survey (10) that quality of workmanship in the appearance of all improvements ranked highest. A professional appearance in the finished product was valued more highly than the project itself.

In general, the cost of renovations that brings a residence up to par with other similar homes in a neighborhood can be nearly recovered at resale; over-enhancements may not be recovered. The results of national surveys are provided as an indication to valuation. These are national averages. Results vary from localities where low cost of construction is available to localities where cost of construction is high.

CHAPTER 3: THE RESIDENTIAL MARKET ANALYSIS

"The deck rule: the space between the boards of a deck should be slightly less than the width of your wife's narrowest heel." Jerry Turem, bureaucrat

INTRODUCTION

The method for determining the worth of a particular residence follows standard criteria. A model for presentation including a blank copy of a worksheet for a residential market analysis is provided online. It would be helpful for you to tear one copy out and keep it in front of you for reference as you go through this chapter. Do not be alarmed by the volume and extensive detail in the following categories. Although you will have to fill in all sections on the worksheet, you will, in all probability, only need to address a small percentage of the information offered in the various categories.

The ratings of good, average, fair or poor have a bearing on the value and the marketability of the property. "Rate each factor in terms of the degree to which you feel it influences how favorably or unfavorably the property compares with competing properties in the same general market area." [11]

Dollar adjustment examples assume an average house under average conditions. Examples of the adjustment process used in a residential market analysis are furnished in Chapter 4. Land valuation is covered in Chapter 5. Explanations of all the terms found on this form are covered in the following:

ADDRESS

Use the street address to designate each property. In rural areas where it would be hard to locate a property by P.O. box number, indicate the road name, the side of the road the property is located on (North, South, East, or West) and the nearest intersection.

PROXIMITY TO THE SUBJECT

Enter distance and direction.

The description of the distance of the comparable properties to your property must be specific (e.g. 2 blocks north or 1.7 mi. SE). If possible, use comparables in your own neighborhood. By doing so, you will be comparing both positive and negative features shared in common. On the other hand, if you live in a historical house, which has added value because of its historical significance, comparable sales may be few and you may have to search much further away than would be normal.

SALES PRICE

Enter the total amount paid by the buyer.

Leave the space blank for subject's home.

The sales price of comparables should be within the same general range of value as your house. A 25% difference in value would raise questions about the validity of the comparison.

DATA SOURCE

Enter the source of data.

The source of sale information may be MLS (multiple listing service), information from the owner, newspapers publishing monthly listings of sales, TRW-REDI property data service (available in print, microfiche or computer download), other sales and tax information gathering services, official records of deeds in the county or city clerk's office, the broker or salespeople involved in the sale, the owners themselves, a record of sales published by a local real estate board, or the tax assessor's office. If there is an indication that the sale is forced (such as a tax sale, foreclosure, or estate liquidation), that property is not comparable and should not be used.

PRICE/GROSS LIVING SPACE

Enter the price per square foot.

Divide the sales price by the gross living area to arrive at the price per square foot of gross living area for the comparables. You will not be able to calculate the price per gross living space for your home until the end, since only then will you be able to determine the price of your home. Be sure to use only heated living space in your calculation. Divide the sales price by the number of square feet of gross living area. For example, if a comparable 2,000 square-foot house sells for $500,000, then $250 is the square foot price of gross living area.

SALES OR FINANCING CONCESSIONS

Enter "None" or a dollar figure.

In practice, this is a little-used adjustment since it is generally not highlighted, the information is more difficult to find and many of those determining the valuation of property simply follow the status quo and do not dig for facts in this particular area. But varying financial terms of sale realistically affect selling prices. If the buyer has assumed the loan at a lower than prevailing rate, the seller has financed the loan at a lower than market price or if the seller makes a cash concession at the time of sale ("buy down"), these arrangements affect the sales price. If you want to take a closer look, follow along.

The comparable sale based on an assumable loan has the below itemized conditions. Assume a prevailing mortgage rate of 10% and a corresponding monthly payment of $1,428.

Purchase Price	$170,000
Down Payment	$20,000
Remaining Principal Balance	$150,000
Interest Rate	8%
Monthly Payments for 20 yrs	$1,242

Divide the monthly payments by the payment required at the current prevailing rate to obtain the percentage to be applied to the principal amount of the loan.

$1,242 / $1,428 = .8697 or 86.97%

Multiply the remaining principal amount of the loan by this percentage to find the adjusted value.

$150,000 x 86.97% = $130,455

By adding the down payment to the adjusted value of the loan, the cash equivalent value of the sale is determined.

$20,000 + $131,955 = **$150,455**

In this example, an $18,000 adjustment in value would be appropriate ($170,000-$150,455 = **$19,545** or $19,500 rounded off).

Other examples of sales or financing concessions are: loan discount points, loan origination fees, closing costs customarily paid by the buyer, payment of condominium or PUD association fees, refunds of (or credit for) the borrower's expense, absorption of monthly payments, assignment of rent payments and the inclusion of non-realty items in the transaction.

The negative adjustments must reflect the difference between what the comparable actually sold for with the sales concession and what it would have sold for without the concession.

DATE OF SALE

Enter the annual assessment date for the subject.

Enter the sales date for the comparables.

For the subject property, the date of sale should always be the annual assessment date for the year that you are appealing. The comparables must always sell <u>before</u> the annual assessment date of the subject.

If you find that the price of housing has declined, let's say by 12% over the last year, a 1% per month adjustment to the comparative sales would be in order. i.e. a $200,000 comparable sold 6 months previous to your annual assessment date would be adjusted $12,000 downwards. See pages 85-86 for a narrative detailing this adjustment.

6 months x 1% x $200,000 = $12,000

Be prepared to have evidence to support this depreciation or inflation rate by a photocopy of that factual study gleaned from multiple listing service data, a news article, industry survey, government statistics, etc. Also comment on the reason(s) for using comparables if they are over 6 months old.

LOCATION

Two comparisons are necessary:

> 1. An overall rating of your home within your neighborhood by indicating "Good", "Average," "Fair" or "Poor."

> 2. Rate the location of each comparable against yours as either "Superior," "Equal" or "Inferior."

Location adjustments for single family homes are related to differences in the values of competing site locations. Also, if the sale property is located in a different neighborhood than the subject, an adjustment may be needed. If a 10% or greater adjustment is required, the sale is not comparable.[12]

Traffic volume is one of the most common problems in residential neighborhoods. Properties close to heavy traffic are less desirable. Traffic conditions may vary from moderate to heavy to severe and, accordingly, be penalized two to three times that of a quieter road.

For instance, a corner lot with a moderately dangerous intersection, increased traffic and noise, may be less desirable than an interior lot and may merit a $6,000 negative adjustment. A property moderately suffering from a T-lot influence (where because of the location of the lot, headlights shine directly into the house at night and privacy is diminished from approaching traffic during the day) may qualify for a $7,000 adjustment. Also, the driveway to the site location must be convenient to the lot and the street, otherwise it would suffer in value.

Site locations can strongly affect the value. Cul-de-sac lots, interior lots, flag lots, corner lots are generally more desirable than T-intersections lots. However, corner lots are usually more valuable but may not be in residential areas having lots 50 feet or more in width. The air of privacy of the corner lot is offset if other lots have distances of 20 or more feet between houses. If the corner lot is on a busy street, it would negatively impact the value.

Types of Lots

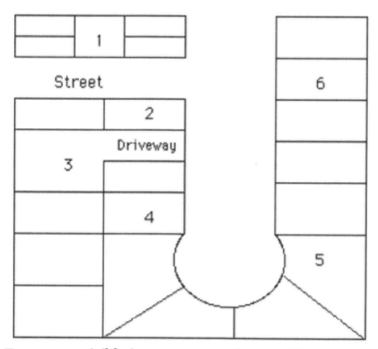

For a more visible image, copy and paste URL:
http://propertytaxax.com/amazon/lottypes.htm

1. **Key Lot** - one side adjoining to the rear of other lots; least desirable lot in a subdivision. When the side of one lot abuts to the rear of other lots with the view of backyards, sheds and garages, there usually results a decrease in value.

2. **Corner Lot** - close to intersection, better access to rear yard, more prominence on a street. Assessors use corner lot influence tables that are structured to give an increase in value for the corner of two streets.

42

These higher assessments may be in error because of: more noise from passing traffic, danger from being close to intersection, possible objectionable noise, headlights, large front yard requires more maintenance (also snow removal in Northern climates), people and dogs short-cut across the lot, fire hydrant and annoying street lamps may be located close by, high EMF electric step-down power transformers often located on intersections and lack of privacy caused by two streets.

3. **Flag Lot** - increased privacy, possibly narrow access, possibly objectionable view of adjoining property's backyard, garage or shed, possibly more driveway clearing costs in colder climates. It can be worth more than other lots in the area if it has a better view of surrounding lots or has more of a driveway.

4. **Interior lot** - a normal lot, usually with small front yard; may have large back yard with increased privacy or small lot with little access to backyard; may have many abutting neighbors with objectionable view. Most people prefer interior lots and most single family homes are located on interior lots.

5. **Cul-de-sac** - premium lot, extra privacy, reduced street traffic, lots are tapered with reduced street frontage requiring limited maintenance, greater safety for small children playing in the street, minimum street parking, minimum front yard privacy.

6. **T-Intersection -** an interior lot that suffers because of its location, lack of privacy, automobile headlights shining into the house at night, noise from increased traffic, increased danger from vehicle failing to turn corner.

On spotting a bad neighborhood: *"If you're in a fast food restaurant that's part of a national chain and the premises are dirty, you're in a very dangerous neighborhood."* Jeff Brown, astronomer

Neighborhoods: Income levels tend to set a value range for a neighborhood. The typical style and design of houses, gross living area, quality and price, along with prevalent lot size, set the general tone for identifying a particular neighborhood. Houses that do not conform to the neighborhood are adjusted for by their specific characteristics (condition, design and appeal, quality, etc.) in the market analysis.

Houses that all look the same (i.e. row houses) suffer in value when compared to other neighborhoods that have more eye-pleasing variations in house design. Neighborhoods that have buildings boarded up, yards taken over by weeds, trash, discarded bottles, broken down cars, or general junk in the yards lack appeal when compared to well-landscaped neighborhoods with a good, healthy general appearance. Homes in developments with well thought-out street layouts, good architecture, pleasant-appearing front yards will command higher prices.

By limiting your comparable search to your neighborhood or neighborhoods that closely approximate yours, you will be comparing like-neighborhood characteristics and, consequently, increase the accuracy of your residential market analysis.

Recreational Facilities: Neighborhoods also can differ by their convenience to shopping centers and the types of recreational facilities available to the residents. If you must choose a different neighborhood because of a lack of comparables in your neighborhood, and if your comparable does not have a social amenity that you possess, then an adjustment in valuation is appropriate. If, for instance, your comparable is located near a park and tennis courts but there is no recreational facility near your location, a downward adjustment for the comparable is in order.

Services: Some services detract when they are too close to a site such as funeral parlors, fire houses, public schools, stores, restaurants, medical offices, motels, etc. The barking dog next door is a curable nuisance and would not qualify; a dog kennel, however, would qualify. By using sales data from similar types of nuisances, you may find that a $10,000 to $20,000 or more adjustment is in order.

Nuisances, such as nuclear power plants, show a depressing effect on the value of land which increases with the age of the plant. [13] Psychological fears increase, land becomes less desirable, and consequently, there is a decrease in the value of the surrounding land and housing. Fannie Mae requires appraisers to, "Consider the present or anticipated use of any adjoining property that may adversely effect the marketability of the subject property." [14]

Employment: Instability and lack of diverse business employment opportunities, even industries hooked to economic cycles (such as defense, auto, tobacco, forest product, etc.), will create market resistance in the mind of a typical buyer. If the distance and time required to travel to employment centers by a neighborhood is inconvenient, costly and/or lack of public transportation exists, then this unfavorable condition influences the value of the neighborhood.

Utilities: If your property is inaccessible or lacks utilities and comparable sale properties do not have this problem, these conditions, too, are reasons for adjustments. The rule is that the property's utilities must meet community standards and be generally accepted by the area residents. Off-site private facilities are acceptable only if the property has access rights and if there is a legal and binding access and maintenance agreement.

Police or Fire Protection: If this is notoriously inadequate, a typical buyer would be less inclined to invest in such a neighborhood.

Taxes: It stands to reason that higher-taxed neighborhoods are less favorable to live in than lower-taxed neighborhoods of equal character. If there is a significant difference in taxes, make an adjustment for the tax difference, assuming the amenities and characteristics of the competing neighborhood are equal.

Special Assessments: These also reduce the value of highly-taxed houses when compared to similar type moderately-taxed homes. They are levied for public improvements such as sewers, sidewalks, garbage collection, etc. Adjustments should be made if certain properties are not equally subject to a special assessment.

Schools: The reputation for good schools or for poor schools affects the values of homes in a neighborhood. Good schools are attractive to families with children and affect the buying patterns of future families considering the community. In an area where children are bussed to schools outside their area, the reputation of the neighborhood school would be less important.

Crime: Violent crimes, burglaries, and robberies have a depressing effect on property values especially in localities accessible to a central city. The crime level in some neighborhoods impact resale values as residents desire to leave and prospective buyers look for safer areas in which to purchase their homes.

Graffiti: Graffiti on buildings may alert everyone to a change in neighborhood boundaries. Prospective buyers are not blind to signs of disregard for private property.

If a location adjustment is necessary because of a difference in neighborhoods, that amount can be determined by <u>matched pairs</u> analysis. This is often a difficult procedure to "pull out of a hat." However, if you are able, find a similar pair of houses alike in all respects (you may have to adjust for minor differences) except that one is in the neighborhood of the subject and the other is in the neighborhood of the comparable. The difference in prices is the adjustment.

LEASEHOLD/FEE SIMPLE

Enter "Fee" if applicable.

Fee simple, sometimes called fee or fee simple absolute, is the greatest possible estate or degree in the right of ownership and continues without time limitation. Most homes are fee estates. An estate is the degree of ownership that a person has in real property.

A leasehold is the right to possess and use real estate for a specific time created by the lease. If there is a leasehold, explain in the addendum the terms and conditions of the lease. Compare like to like; use fee comparables or lease comparables.

SITE

(refer to Chapter 5: Land Valuation for more detail)

1. Enter the size of the lot. One acre = 43,560 square feet. You can give your site measurements in acres or in square feet; just be consistent in your description.

2. Enter overall rating of "Good," "Average," "Fair" or "Poor."

3. Enter comparable rating of "Superior," "Equal" or "Inferior."

A site is land that is prepared for a contemplated purpose and may contain improvements such as utilities, grading and a driveway. It addresses the confines of the property. This is the area to make adjustments for "legal" or "illegal" compliance with zoning regulations, utilities' presence or absence, site improvements such as curbs, gutters, sidewalks, street lights, etc. Also, size and shape of lot, topography, drainage and soil conditions, landscaping, driveway, easements, encroachments, zoning restrictions and any detrimental conditions are adjusted for in this section.

Try to locate and find similar sq. ft. property sites, with similar shape, slope, drainage, landscaping and street features. In some areas, differences of 30% in site size may reflect a small adjustment in value; it depends on overall size and location. 100% difference in size does not indicate your property is twice as valuable as a similar property if it is not sub-dividable and may reflect only a 20% addition in land value.

Determining the market value for the land is difficult in built-up areas where no recent land sales have occurred. Even in rural areas, recent land cost data may be hard to come by. Usually the value of the property is not disputed in property tax appeals since most of the value is placed on the house. Rather than cover land valuation at great length, the "4-3-2-1" rule of land valuation is offered below. This rule is the basis for all land valuation tables. Further information on land valuation is provided in Chapter 5.

Depth tables assist in valuation in lot depth, however the least complex basis for computing valuation is the "4-3-2-1 rule." This rule states that the first 25% of depth of a lot represents 40% of its total value, the second 25% of depth represents 30% of value, the third 25% represents 20% of the total value, and the fourth and last 25% of the site depth represents 10% of the total value. [15] More complex depth tables are relied on by tax assessors. However, "...complex depth tables not only give the mistaken appearance of unverified accuracy, but are also difficult to explain to clients and courts: any error attributable to the use of the cruder computations is probably minor in the final analysis." [16]

If the total cost of the lot is $100,000, then the first 25 feet is worth $40,000, the second 25 feet is worth $30,000, the third 25 feet is worth $20,000 and the last 25 feet is worth $10,000.

"4-3-2-1" Land Valuation Table

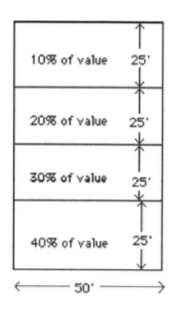

For a more visible image, copy and paste URL:
http://propertytaxax.com/amazon/4321.htm

The table shows that if a lot had 50-feet frontage and only 25-feet depth, it would be valued at 40% that of a lot 50-foot wide and 100-feet deep. If the lot were 50-feet wide and 50-feet deep, it would be valued at 70% when compared to a lot 50-feet wide and 100-feet deep. If the lot were 50-ft. x 75-ft., it would be valued at 90% when compared to a lot 50-ft. wide and 100-ft. deep.

The mathematics follow from the "4-3-2-1" Rule. You'll have to "chop" up the land into 4-quarters. Each quarter is valued accordingly.

Example: Property A is 50-feet x 100-feet totaling 5,000 square feet and sold for $100,000. Property B is located immediately next to Property A and was similar in all respects but was only 50-feet x 75-feet. It's value would be approximately 10% less ($90,000) even though the property is 25% smaller in size.

Example: Property A is 100-feet x 100-ft. valued at $100,000. Property B is 100-feet x 125-feet. How much is property B worth using the 4-3-2-1 rule?

Answer: Property A is 10,000-sq. ft. Property B is 12,500-sq. ft. and is 2,500-sq. ft. larger than Property A. That extra 2,500-sq. ft. is valued at $10,000 (falls inside the 25% range valued at 10% for our control Property A valuation for $100,000 = additional $10,000 or $110,000 total valuation for property B).

Again, "chop" up the land into 4-quarters. Value each quarter accordingly.

Example: Property A is 25-ft. x 120-ft. totaling 3,049-sq.ft. and sold for $68,000. The square foot value is $22.30/sq. ft. Property B is 30-ft. x 130-ft. totaling 3,920 sq.ft. What is the value of Property B?

Property B looks is in the last 25% "chop" that gets a 10% valuation (actual figure is 19.8%). The rule says it adds only 10% more value to the property. $68,000 + $6,800 = $74,800 ([(.10 x $68,000)] + $68,000)

Since the front footage of Lot A is similar to Lot B, the difference in size is negligible. Buildable lots in many municipalities vary in geometry and size and finding equivalent lot sizes for comparison is nearly impossible. If the property was twice as large, the value of Lot B may be only 20% more. It's that simple using the "4-3-2-1" Rule.

If your lot is superior to the comparable lot, add a dollar amount as an equalizing adjustment. If your lot is inferior to the comparable, deduct a dollar amount for an equalizing adjustment. Small differences in lot size usually are not reasons for an adjustment.

Many waterfront lots and lots in prime city business locations are another story all together. Front footage would be a more viable method for divining market value. You can use the front footage method but it may not be as accurate an approximation of value as the 4-3-2-1 method. To get academic about accuracy, use the "Matched Pairs Extraction" method to isolate the best result.

To gain the best advantage in their argument, many use the method that sheds more favorable light to their point of view. Tax assessors and mortgage companies want to see a high valuation, appealers a low one.

Overview For Assigning Values To Lots

When one get's the "sold listings", only the **total price for the home is given**. It is not broken down for lot value and house value. The tax assessor, on the other hand, comes up with a value for the house and a guesstimate for the lot.

When doing an appraisal, the specific adjustments that effect the lot (slope, location, noise levels, view ... etc.) should be taken against the lot. Most of the adjustment are usually made against the house. For practical purposes, most developed areas have few recent sold vacant lot data points to obtain a large enough sample for estimating a lots value. When one does an appraisal for a vacant lot, then one has to obtain recent sold data points from recently sold lots to make an educated comparable analysis.

So when estimating property (house and lot) value for a tax appeal, one makes adjustments against the figures the assessor assigns.

In real life when doing an appraisal, one does not come up with a figure for the property and then the house. It is not broken down that way. Again, property data points are complicated when a home is place on the property since many factors and influences go into WHY the home sold for what it did. Only the magician tax assessor seems to be able to pull figures and assign lot values out of his hat.

As a matter of practicality, we don't come up with the lot's value, the tax assessor does. Our only data point is a sold price for a house. We'll need to distribute the **final adjusted market value** and assign a portion of it to lot value and house value. This will not make much of a difference since, after we win the case, the tax assessor may juxtapose and assign a different value to lot and house.

The important element is the quality of recently sold comparables that are closest to the subject property in location, time of sale, and square footage.

Site Criteria

Slope: In defining slope (deviation of a surface from horizontal) the following descriptions apply:

> 0-2% nearly level
> 3%-8% gently sloping
> 9%-15% moderately sloping or rolling
> 16%-30% strong sloping or hilly
> 31%-45% steep
> 45% + very steep

If the topography is unacceptable (very uneven terrain) in your market area and an adjustment is necessary, use pictures in your addendum as backup. Sloped and hill lots can be classified as top-of-hill, bottom-of-hill, uphill, downhill and side-of-hill lots. It is not unusual to spend 25% or more of the sloped lot's value in backfill and grading costs.

Top-of-Hill Lot - most desirable location, top of hill may vary from a gently sloping to a very steep classification, 360 degree view, building can be situated to maximize southern exposure, view, access, etc., lot drains well, excellent TV and radio reception, may have problems with steep driveways, icy conditions and snow removal.

Bottom-of-Hill Lot - least desirable location at base of hill, traffic going uphill can be noisy, possible drainage problems from lots above during rain or snow-melts, may be a more hazardous location because of bad weather, limited uphill view, road dust and debris.

Uphill Lot - is uphill from the access road (the access road leads directly to the house). Slopes may be 3-45% or more, drains well, house appears larger and more im-pressive, may have problems with water runoff from above situated lots, possible steep driveway and snow and ice removal problems, may lack privacy, possible traffic noise.

Downhill Lot - is situated downhill from the access road on slopes ranging from 3-45% or more, affords more privacy, house looks smaller than it is, chance of auto veering down from road into residence; if steep, driveway ice and snow removal problems, road dust and debris.

Side-Hill Lot - is a lot that is sloped away (usually 15% or less) at the side of a street or road and has the same general view as surrounding side-hill lots, lot drains well, two-story house may block view, may have steep driveway, icy conditions, snow removal problems.

Additional Site Criteria

Off-Site Drainage: HUD guidelines state, "All drainage must be away from the structure. A minimum fall of six inches from the structure by 10 feet should be achieved except as restricted by side lot lines or other major considerations." [17] Top soil layered over a clay laced base may not drain necessitating expensive drainage. If the drainage is inadequate, be sure to explain and make an adjustment reflecting the drainage correction (its cost).

Hazards and Nuisances (Natural and Manmade): HUD calls special attention to unscreened hazards (dangerous road intersections, unprotected railroad rights of way, high voltage transmission lines, excavations, retention basins, ponds, drainage canals and other facilities).

1. "No dwelling should be located closer than 300 feet from the site boundary of an active or planned drilling site.

2. No structure in a single-family subdivision can be within 75 feet of an actual operating well without proper mitigation measures. Operating wells should be fenced and permanently screened.

3. Housing must be at least 300 feet from abandoned wells unless a letter is procured from a responsible authority within the State government that the well was safely and permanently abandoned.

4. Dwellings and related improvements may not be located within an easement of a high-voltage transmission line.

55

5. Dwellings and related property improvements cannot be located within the fall distance of any pole, tower, or support structure of a radio/TV transmission tower, microwave relay tower, etc.

6. Dangerous Natural Hazards (faults, sinkholes). A specific site is not acceptable with these conditions present.

7. Incompatible land uses such as industrial activities, treatment plants, etc. Lots in close proximity to these activities are not acceptable.

8. Oil and high-pressure gas lines. Any part of a residential structure must be at least ten feet from the outer boundary of the pipeline easement of a high-pressure gas line and liquid petroleum transmission lines. New construction also requires a certification of compliance with Title 49, Transportation Code of Federal Regulations for the area 220 yards on either side of the center-line of high pressure transmission lines." [18]

Zoning: Changes in zoning may increase the value of a property substantially. Always use the highest and best use value for the property. If the existing house still contributes to the overall value of the total property, is legally authorized, financially feasible and physically possible, then it continues to have appropriateness as a residential valuation (as opposed to a commercial valuation if vacant).

Zoning compliance can be legal conforming, legal nonconforming or illegal. If a property is grandfathered (improvements existed before the zoning regulation) and does not comply with current zoning requirements (i.e. size of home, lot size, set back requirements, etc.), an adjustment may be in order. The reason is that if the home was destroyed by fire, hurricane or natural disaster, the current building code may only allow a smaller, less expensive house to occupy the site. Variances are special exceptions granted by zoning boards to allow nonconforming construction.

There may be restrictions or limitations placed on your property in the form of unfavorable zoning ordinances or restrictions created by private owners. These clauses in deeds, agreements or even in plans of a subdivision are called restrictive covenants and may qualify for an adjustment.

A failure to enforce zoning ordinances can cause a decrease in value of homes in a neighborhood. For example, many illegal mother-daughter homes used for two families' income or for business located in residential zones may create traffic congestion, traffic hazards, and increased stress on a neighborhood.

Encroachments: These result when improvements extend onto another's property. The cost of removal is considered in determining the adjustment.

Easement: An easement is the right or privilege that one has to use land for a specific purpose, i.e. a right of way for pipes, utility poles, private or public passage, historic and view easement, mineral and mining easement. If an easement exists on your property, it will impose a negative influence.

Landscaping: Generally, most comparables are similar in the area of landscaping and driveways, but there are exceptions. According to Richard M. Rhodes, M.A.I., and member of the American Institute of Real Estate Appraisers, a front lawn will add 1%, a front and back lawn will add 2%, shade trees and landscaping effects will add another 2-5% in value.

Majestic trees will add 2% to 10%. The maximum value added to a house and lot by lush landscaping is 10%. Rock, stone or paving work can add up to 5% in value (about half the contract price for the type of pavement constructed). [19] Exotic trees and shrubs used to landscape a low-quality home may be considered an over-improvement but would be justified in a good-quality home.

If a mature shade tree adds 10% to the value of a lot, you cannot add 20% to the lot if it has two trees, 30% if it contains 3 trees. [20] Landscaping that does not conform to a neighborhood may be viewed as undesirable and may lack appeal. Typical value ranges in many average neighborhoods for landscaping range from $500-$3,000.

Driveways: they may be constructed of gravel, asphalt, concrete, poly-pebble, interlocking brick blocks, etc. and may vary in price. Driveways that do not have a turn around, where backing up into the street is dangerous, may be cause for adjustment.

Driveways with additional paving or circular driveways may not bring large added value in all neighborhoods. A paved driveway adjustment may range from $1,000-$4,000 or more, depending on size. Use pictures, estimates from landscapers, paving contractors, real estate agents, etc. in an attached addendum to support your adjustments.

Waterfront Homes: The value of a waterfront home is greatly influenced by the location, view, size and shape of the body of water, the water acidity (important for fish yield and abundance of underwater vegetation), depth, clarity, and type of shoreline. A significant difference in price results from a shallow water site as compared to a deep water site. Older lakes with less than 15-foot depth are usually muck ridden and less in demand.

Other financial considerations may result from seaweed accumulation due to an unfavorable location, noise from passing boats or boat "hang-outs", sandbars, if home is in compliance with sewer or septic regulations, type of water bottom (sandy, rocky, muddy, sharp drop-off or gentle slope). Island locations with bridge or ferry access differ considerably in valuation from inaccessible locations.

Access to a main body of water may be limited by low bridges and narrow passage ways disqualifying the location for harboring sailboats, party boat or larger canopied boats. Such is typical of many waterways. This type of lakefront location is less desirable than a location on the main body of water. Depending on locations, as much as a 30% decrease in valuation may apply.

Even if a stream crosses a portion of the property, an additional 5% to 10% addition to property value may be in order. Use comparable sales from the same body of water that are most similar to the subject's situation. When photographing the front of a lakefront home, the front faces the lake and the back faces the street.

Floating docks are another issue to address. If a dock is not permanent, it is classified as chattel and not subject to tax. Chattel is an item of personal property which is movable, as distinguished from real property (land and unmovable improvements). Often, though, floating docks are taxed as permanent docks. Permanent docks require building permits, sometimes easements. Often restrictions apply as to length and breadth.

Boathouses are a valuable asset. Often there are severe limitations to size or legislation that does not allow additional boathouses to be built on a body of water. Depending on the construction, pre-existing boathouses can be extremely valuable (because of the grand fathering) especially if building restrictions are in effect.

59

Historical matched pairs of homes with and without boathouses would establish value.

Shore Homes: The seashore home is greatly influenced by the width of the beach. Shore erosion can have a devastating effect on price. Sand reclamation projects may add shorefront to your comparables, thereby increasing value. Increased beach width is protection against storm surge and flooding of low areas.

A multiple regression analysis study along a 60-mile stretch of beach in South Carolina covering two different communities demonstrated an increase of house value by 2.6% for an increase in beach width of 10%. For up to one half mile from the ocean this proportional adjusted shore front-to-house value held true. For instance a 3-foot shore front home vs. a 30-foot shore front home would increase a property by 26%.[21]

Floodplains: If property is prone to flooding, has poor drainage or if wetlands are located on the property, this would be a cause for a lower assessment. To determine if you are in a flood hazard area, consult Flood Insurance Rate Maps (FIRM) put out by the Federal Emergency Management Agency. They are found in most major libraries or you can write or call:

Federal Emergency Management Agency Flood Map Distribution Center 6930 (A-F) San Tomas Road Baltimore, MD 21227-6227	Continental U.S. 1-800-638-6620 Maryland only 1-800-492-6605 Alaska, Hawaii, 1-800-638-6831

Floodplain elevations change and not all floods occur within 100-year flood boundaries. "Note: The term '100-year flood' does not mean that a flood will occur once in every 100 years, but rather that there is a 1% or greater chance that a flood level will be equal or exceeded in any given year."[22]

What is most important in determining the value for property located in areas of floodplains is "the average person's perception" of the possibility of the property flooding. The memory of a recent flood would dramatically undercut property values. If raised foundations or similarly engineered improvements are allowed, the additional costs of these improvements could be construed as an adjustment.

Understandably, flood insurance may not always be available, so lack of financing is a major cause for a reduction in valuation. In qualifying communities where private insurance is unavailable, the National Flood Insurance Program provides flood insurance to flood-prone properties. In floodplain situations, valuation of similar-type sold properties in the floodplain is the best determination of value since their sales price will reflect the demerits of that location. If there is a large insurance premium difference between houses in and out of the flood hazard zone, make adjustments to reflect this difference.

Wetlands: Wetlands generally include swamps, marshes, bogs, and similar areas such as sloughs, wet meadows, river overflows, mud flats, and natural ponds. New construction is not allowed in these areas.[23] Note that property classified wetlands may not always be wet due to seasonal changes. The Federal Wetland legislation in Section 404 of the Clean Water Act (33 U.S.F. 1251 et seq.) requires that a permit be obtained from the U.S. Army Corps of Engineers if any alteration is done to the Wetlands.

Failure to determine the presence of a wetland may have drastic consequences to the value of a property. If one alters the wetland without a permit by dredging or filling activities, leveling land or clearing land along waterways, levies, dikes or dams, there may be a significant change to the sellability and therefore the value of the property.

Earthquakes, landslides: If the property is subject to erosion, landslides, unusual fire danger or is located on a major earthquake fault or by a dangerous ravine, then these conditions also affect valuation. Even the strong possibility of an event occurring such as the earthquake of 7.5 magnitude which struck the Coachella Valley area in Palm Springs, CA has decreased land values.[24]

The San Fernando Valley earthquake (Jan. 17, 1994) with a magnitude of 6.7 epicentered in Northridge, CA, caused 61 deaths and $20 billion in damages. The perceived danger of earthquake damage or physical injury near the epicenter will influence property value for years into the future.

See: www.conservation.ca.gov for more information.

Environmental Factors

Valuation of Contaminated Properties: With the existence of Real Estate Disclosure Laws, all aspects of any property come into full view and scrutiny at the time of sale. A knowledgeable buyer will discount any negative areas. It would be foolish to overpay your property taxes by not taking your property's liability into consideration.

Cleanup costs, cost of liability prevention and any attorney's legal fees constitute the direct cost of renewing contaminated property. Other market factors such as, impaired financing costs and other intangible market factors, represent the stigma of increased risk. By putting dollar values on these risks, you will arrive at market value. "This quantification of risk is the precondition necessary for contaminated or previously contaminated properties to regain their marketability." [25]

www.eli.org/about/disclosure.htm a site dedicated to state and local disclosure laws and home to Center for Public Health and Law.

Toxic Contaminants

Drinking Water: In many situations, you cannot sell a home unless environmental problems are corrected. The reason for making an adjustment is that the marketability of your property has suffered and will not sell for the same price as another property not located near or affected by an economic ill.

One in five Americans drinks water that is not adequately treated for toxic chemicals, bacteria, parasites and other pollutants. Environmental Protection Agency (EPA) data indicates that nearly 50 million people are drinking improperly treated water.[26]

Over 700 toxic compounds have been identified by the EPA. There are an estimated 16,000 city landfills, 76,000 industrial landfills and 1.2 million underground gasoline storage tanks that are likely to leak. Steel tanks will corrode.[27] 2,000 out of 50,000 toxic waste sites affect the health of people living nearby according to the EPA.

In regard to the threat of toxic contamination to real estate values, an environmental publication stated, "... aggregate loss could well exceed 10% of the total U.S. real estate value."[28] That figure may seem high, but, more importantly, winning reductions in assessments due to toxic contamination will underline the health risks in understandable dollar terms to responsible authorities.

63

Environmental groups say "millions of people drink water that contains harmful levels of arsenic, radon and chlorine byproducts. Only California has a right-to-know law on making available water quality information."[29] Many counties suffer from heavily pesticide-contaminated groundwater. The EPA found that of the water systems in violation of EPA standards, over 90% were in smaller water systems serving less than 3,300 people. In a study examining the values of 708 single-family homes located within a 2-mile proximity to the Anoka Regional Landfill in Ramsay, MN, results showed a 12% reduction in property values along the landfill boundary and a 6% reduction in property values one mile from the boundary.

The proximity of a neighborhood or any part of it to a hazard or nuisance can affect value.[30] Property within a mile of sites listed in the EPA's National Priority List and the state CERCLA (Comprehensive Environmental Response, Compensations and Liability Act) and/or other state or local lists of hazardous waste sites may be a potential problem and reason for a property tax adjustment.

Point-of-use reverse osmosis units installed under the sink, carbon filtration systems and devices using distillation or ultraviolet light technology can be bought for under $1,000. If the water is suspect, enter an adjustment.

PCB's: Polychlorinated biphenyl's (PCB's) found in leaking fluorescent lighting and electrical transformers or other toxic chemical leakage can also affect your water quality. Soil contaminants are spread by runoff into wells, streams or adjacent land, and further leaching occurs as the contaminants are flushed through the soil. Underground storage tanks, nearby hazardous waste sites, land fills, run off from existing or prior

64

storage/delivery facilities, such as gas stations, oil suppliers, paint or chemical manufacturers, agricultural pollution, acid mine drainage, infectious medical wastes, may be a reason for a property tax reduction. If water is suspect, enter an adjustment.

Nitrate Poisoning: This toxin from excessive use of fertilizers has been found in groundwater not only in the mid-West, but in regional farming communities throughout the United States. Herbicides and pesticides show up in the groundwater and well water. Ultimately your garden vegetables are contaminated. The EPA states that 3% of domestic grown food and 6% of imported food exceed legal tolerance levels for pesticide residues. Researchers at Cornell University found that 60% or more wells in rural areas contain unsafe levels of one or more poisons.[31] Nearly two out of three water systems were repeat violators of EPA nitrate standards over the last 10 years.[32]

Septic Tanks: An improper working septic or neighbor's septic may also be a cause for contamination. Any source of contamination to the drinking water affects the value of the property and should be adjusted for.

Oil Storage Tanks: Even buried home heating oil storage tanks can be a potentially explosive liability problem. It is estimated that a large percentage of tanks over ten years old are leaking and clean-up costs of over $25,000 are not uncommon. The EPA estimates that "as many as two million of the more than five million underground storage tanks in the United States may be leaking." [33] Closure activities requiring soil sampling, contaminated soil disposal and regulatory reporting normally costs $4,000-$7,000.[34] Change in usage, stressed vegetation, or unusual smells may warrant further investigation.

Tank inspections for 1,000 gallons or less cost about $500. If you have an underground oil storage tank and your comparables do not, an inspection fee and an insurance fee for leak liability adjustments are in order. Home sale disclosure laws will reveal any irregularities and any knowledgeable buyer will insist on a test.

Asbestos, Lead, UFFI: Building codes and government regulations outlawed asbestos insulation in 1979. In 1986 other asbestos products such as roofing tiles, pipes, etc. were banned. Construction prior to these dates have a higher probability of having asbestos products than buildings constructed after these dates.

If you have asbestos, especially pipe coverings (which look like white corrugated cardboard or hard plaster inside a paper wrapping), heating/hot water unit coverings, asbestos tile, asbestos siding or other asbestos products, an estimate for its removal should be obtained and a market price adjustment should be made.

In the matter of asbestos contamination, an appeal to the Appellate Division of the State Supreme Court in 1992 ruled in favor of the property taxpayer, "The presumption of validity of an assessment by the taxing authority is rebutted where, as here, credible evidence to the contrary is received." Also, the owners got a tax refund.[35]

Lead Paint: This was commonly used between 1940 and 1980 and must be removed from a house to ensure its sellability. It was not until 1980 that lead paint was prohibited in new construction. This can result in thousands of dollars in adjustment savings, making your house equitable to comparable sale homes in your area. It may cost $5,000- $10,000 to have lead paint removed from your walls and to restore the walls to a condition equal to a comparably located property.

Lead in Drinking Water: The EPA safety level for lead in drinking water is set at 20 micrograms per liter equivalent to 5 ppb (parts per billion), yet an estimated 42 million people may be consuming high levels of lead.

Recently, The EPA Office of Drinking Water has proposed regulations under the Safe Drinking Water Act (SDWA) that establish a maximum contaminant level for lead in drinking water of five micrograms per liter and a maximum contaminant level goal of zero.[36] The EPA found unacceptable lead levels in over 800 municipal water systems.

Drinking water can be contaminated by lead water main pipes or lead solder combined with copper pipe where galvanic corrosion between the two metals releases relatively large amounts of lead into the water. Heat in the hot water supply increases the leaching process of lead to even higher levels. Contact local, county or state health or environmental departments for information about qualified testing laboratories.

The cost for replacing lead soldered plumbing may be significant. Bring your home's value in line with a comparable home that doesn't suffer lead contamination by adjusting for the cost of removing the contamination.

UREA Formaldehyde (UFFI): This foam insulation used as a building material from 1970-1982 is another product that also warrants removal. Urea formaldehyde gives off noxious odors, toxic fumes and is a respiratory irritant. The cost of removal and any replacement to the sheetrock, siding or cosmetic alterations is the adjustment necessary to reflect the market prices of comparable homes to the contaminated home.

Electromagnetic Radiation (EMRs): Anytime an electric current runs through a wire, it produces an electromagnetic field (EMF).

Electric Field: is present if an appliance is on or off.
-Measured in volts/meter (v/m).
-Produced by electric charges in power lines, lights, appliances.
-Pushes and pulls charged particles (ions) in the direction of the field.
-Voltage remains constant.
-Is easily screened, little passes through walls of house or skin.

Magnetic Field: will disappear when an appliance is shut off.
-Measured in amps/meter (amp/m) or most often in units called gauss.
-Measured with gaussmeters or magnetometers
-Results from the motion of charges in the electric field (current).
-Results from the motion of current and fluctuates with that current.
-The stronger the current, the stronger the magnetic field.
-Peak usage times cause large increases in magnetic fields
-Pushes charged particles (ions) perpendicular to their direction of motion
-Travels through most matter without losing strength

An estimated 10 million acres of land and one million homes in the United States lie close enough to transmission lines that the EMF levels on the property exceed the average household background levels. Public concern over power-line EMFs may decrease the value of this property. One recently published analysis estimates that the total economic cost of the EMF controversy exceeds one billion dollars annually.(37)

Electromagnetic Fields: This refers to magnetic and electric fields lumped together as one and can be a source of informational confusion; sometimes intentional, sometimes accidentally. The earth has a natural 500 mG DC magnetic field; it makes compasses work. An AC field is another matter. AC or alternating current is produced by making the current move back and forth 60 times a second (60 Hz.) It is this AC electromagnetic field that, in some studies, has been tied in to leukemia, cancer deaths and other adverse health implications.

Epidemiological studies are centered on children in order to rule out preexisting factors. Adults are equally at risk. The central study in electronic fields (EMF) was conducted over a 23-year period (from 1950-1973) by Wertheimer and Leeper. They concluded that the children who lived in high-exposure homes with magnetic fields ranging from 2 to 2.6 mG (close to power transmission lines) were 2 to 3 times as likely to contract some form of cancer (specifically leukemia, lymphomas and nervous system tumors) than children who did not live close to power transmission lines (homes with low EMF readings).(38)

Another more recent study by Savitz as part of the New York State Power Lines Project (which was done with the thought to disprove Wertheimer and Leepers results) merely confirmed and better defined exposure criteria to EMFs and its link to cancer. The average field in high-current homes was 2-3 mG resulting in twice the risk for specific cancers. He found the same double risk for children living near high-current distribution lines. Children who lived in homes exposed to the highest currents were five times more likely to get cancer.(39)

69

Tomenius measured the proximity of high-voltage power lines (6,000-200,000 volts), transmission lines and other high current sources to childhood cancers in Sweden. He took the measurement from the front door of the children's houses and found that with intensities of 3 mG or above, those children were twice as likely to die of cancer.[40]

Other studies also showed increased cancer death rates for people living near radio or T.V. broadcast transmitters, microwave towers and radar beams from airports. Conditions of high blood pressure, chronic stress effects, chronic fatigue, changes in white and red blood cell count, increased metabolism, headaches, memory loss and brain damage have been associated with high EMF's in other studies.

115 kV-756 kV power transmission lines can show a 5 mG readings at ranges from 100-2,000 feet. Also at risk are homes within 120 feet of: large gauge primary distribution wires, 6 or more thin wires, first or second home close to step down transformer, within 60 ft of 3-5 thin primary wires.[41] Also, improperly wired 3-way wall switches in the home and mistakes in wiring subpanels (not balancing the hot and neutral loads) cause high magnetic fields.

While there is no established standard for a "safe" exposure limit to EMFs, the arbitrary **2 mG** level used in epidemiological studies shows statistical relevance. Excessive EMF levels can be tested for by your local utility company (usually for free) using extremely low frequency (ELF) magnetic field meters. These instruments are also known as ELF Gaussmeters and can be purchased upward from $100.

In 1993, 9 million dollars were spent in government-conducted tests to determine the harmful effects, if any,

70

from EMFs. Through numerous studies on laboratory rats, no statistical relevance to disease was uncovered. Nevertheless, the perceived cancer risk resulting from a proximity to a high EMF source(s) would definitely have a depressing influence on the resale value of EMF contaminated property especially if the person buying the house was informed that it had high EMF readings and by moving into the house they could significantly increase their chances of disease and cancer death. With the ever increasing journalistic coverage of EMFs, the perceived contamination by the buying public will have a depressing effect on visually suspect, EMF-contaminated real estate. Fear affects purchasing decisions and where people choose not to live.

In a relative case the New York Court of Appeals ruled in favor of a claimant stating that, "Whether the danger is scientifically genuine or verifiable fact should be irrelevant to the central issue of its market value impact."(42) The judge cited another case,..."As the Court of Appeals of Kansas has noted, 'Logic and fairness...dictate that any loss of market value proven with a reasonable degree of probability should be compensable, regardless of its source.'(43)

If no one will buy a residential lot because it has a high-voltage line across it, the lot is a total loss even though the owner has the legal right to build a house on it. If buyers can be found, but only at half the value it had before the line was installed, the owner has suffered a 50% loss."(44)

See Residential Market Analysis Example #5 for an EMF adjustment example.

Radon: Radon is a tasteless, odorless, colorless gas that is a product of uranium decay. Different types of rocks and soil contain various amounts of uranium and all have some potential for radon release. Radon is measured in

PICOCURIES per liter (pCi/l) which is equivalent to one trillionth of a curie for one liter of air. Radon enters a home when there is a pressure difference.

Even a 1/100 of 1% difference would cause air to move from a high-pressure to a low-pressure region (the same principle behind why the wind blows). Average soil radon gas in the United States is 100 pCi/l so it is easy to see why radon gas can enter by cracks between the floor and walls, openings around pipes, drains, cracks in concrete, and openings of any kind.

According to the EPA, one in twelve homes (6 million) are above 4 pCi/l and some action should be taken to reduce radon concentration levels. The Washington Post printed, "Scientists believe that radon is responsible for as many as 20,000 lung cancer deaths each year." A New York Times article revealed that radon "may endanger 8 million homes."

Figures for fatalities from indoor radon range from 8,000 to 30,000 per year according to the EPA and NRC. Radon decay products are the largest source of radiation exposure. "Homes with concentrations 10-100 times the average occur with startling frequency. Long-term occupants run a risk of developing lung cancer as high as that from heavy cigarette smoking.(45)

Energy-efficient homes increase the risk of cancer from radon gas. For example, an energy-efficient home may be equivalent to one air change per 10 hours, whereas an inefficient home may have 2 air changes per hour. The more time one spends in a radon contaminated home, the greater one's exposure. By-products of radon attach themselves to small dust particles (aerosols) which are breathed in and lodge in the lungs. These dust particles stay trapped in the lungs for as long as 30 minutes and damage sensitive cells by injurious radioactive radiation.

Radioactive alpha particles pass through cell walls and cause multiple breaks in the DNA chain. When the cells repair the damaged DNA, they do so incorrectly and abnormal cells result giving way to tumorous cells. Smokers are even more at risk. Of the smokers who died of cancer, death rates as high as 1:3 may be attributable to radon and there is no telling how many deaths were caused by passive smoke.[46]

The National Research Council estimates that in the United States, at least 21,800 fatal lung cancers per year are due to indoor radon, and 6% of U.S. homes contain dangerous levels of radon.[47] Radon levels vary in any given house. In summer, windows tend to be opened and in winter the home is closed up.

The EPA has determined that **4 pCi/l** is the level at which you should be concerned for your health. 4 pCi/l is equivalent to smoking 1/2 pack of cigarettes a day resulting in a death rate of 2 persons per 100 population. 2 pCi/l is equivalent to having 100 chest x-rays each year and results in a death rate of l person per 100 population.[48] Methods to reduce radon include ventilating the basement, sealing cracks, holes, and joints in the basement walls and floor, installing a system of pipes, drain tiles with fans, etc.

About 10,000 pCi/l of radon in water is equivalent to l pCi/l of radon in the air. The average concentration of radon in ground water is 5,000 pCi/liter with levels as high as 200,000 pCi/l for granite areas in Maine.[49] One in twenty homes that gets water from private wells has excessively high radon water levels (about 2 million people affected).

Water systems that are from reservoirs or water purification systems contribute to a low level of radon since this allows time for dissipation (radon has a half-life of 4 days). 20% of the population who use individual wells or small community water systems are over the 4 pCi/l level of exposure. Radon is released when pressure is reduced, temperature is increased or water is aerated. Therefore, the largest release of radon occurs when taking a shower or a bath, in dishwashers and washing machines. Even a cornfield releases 3 times the amount of radon as compared to the bare soil.(50)

The National Academy of Sciences affirms that the risk of lung cancer from inhaling radon is three to twelve times that of stomach cancer from consumed radiated water. A granulated activated charcoal filtering unit that is used for reduction of radon levels in water, costs from $800 to $2,000 for treatment in the 50,000 pCi/l to 150,000 pCi/l range.

An Associated Press release in March 1994 stated that, according to the EPA, the average family water bills would have to be increased by as much as $242 per year in community water systems in order to reduce the radon in drinking water supplied by underground wells.

In 1988, Congress passed a radon bill whose long-term goal was to reduce the indoor radon levels to 0.2-0.5 pCi/l. Effective July 29, 1994, the House in Washington passed legislation where home sellers have to tell prospective buyers the results if the building has been tested for radon. Radon mitigation of a high-radon contaminated home ranges from $1,000-$7,000+. Due to the negative psychological market resistance to high radon levels, the cost of eliminating the presence of radon to your homestead should constitute the equalizing adjustment.

http://www.nsc.org The National Safety Council located in Washington, D.C. offers a short term radon detection kit and a long-term radon detection test kit to test the air quality of your home.

Noise, Traffic: Decibels measure how loud a noise is; every 8 decibel difference sounds roughly twice as loud to the human ear. Hearing damage from very loud noises worsens with longer exposure.

Noise in Decibels Relative to Noise Source

Quiet Whispers	20 decibels
Conversations At Home	50 decibels
Vacuum Cleaner	70 decibels
Dishwasher, Garbage Disposer	80-95 decibels
Lawn Mower, Jackhammer	100 decibels
Chain Saw	110 decibels
Jet Takeoff	130-150 decibels

Source: Temple University and the U.S. Environmental Protection Agency

A survey of noise levels from 13 studies covering 17 airports concerning noise disturbance levels to people was published indicating the following results.(52)

Low = 60-65 Ldn or decibels (62.5 Ldn as midpoint of range)
Moderate = 65-70 Ldn or decibels (67.5 Ldn as midpoint of range)
Substantial = 70-75 Ldn or decibels (72.5 Ldn as midpoint of range)
Severe = 75-80 Ldn and above (77.5 Ldn as midpoint)

Studies by appraisers determining the reduction in property value on the level of noise found a 0.58% reduction in property value per decibel increase in the noise level over 60 Ldn or decibels.[53] The following mean values were arrived at:

Noise Level to Market Value Correlation

Noise Level	Low	Moderate	Substantial	Severe
Decibels or Ldn.	65.5 Ldn.	67.5 Ldn.	72.5 Ldn.	77.5 Ldn.
Reduction in Market Value	1.4%	4.3%	7.2%	10.2%

"Noise (is defined as that) which interferes with normal activities such as sleeping, conversation, or recreation. The noise causes actual physical harm or adversely affects mental health. Sound levels in excess of 75 decibels are not acceptable for proposed construction. Sound levels within 65 to 76 decibels may be acceptable with sound lessening measures such as air conditioning, extra insulation, etc."[54]

HUD will not accept proposed construction cases and existing dwellings less than one year old if the property is located within Runway Clear Zones at Civil Airports or Clear Zones or Accident Potential Zone 1 at Military Airfields. Call the airport, county, town or D.O.T. (Department of Transportation) to identify these conditions.[55]

Noise sources should be photographed and exact distances must be given for those noise sources which are in close proximity to the site. If your property is plagued with excessive road noise, heavy truck traffic, close to airplane landing and take-off patterns, train noise, proximity to industrial noise, noise from a rock quarry or mining operation, then an adjustment should be made to reduce your tax burden.

Noise that is physically annoying becomes a quality-of-life issue. Unnecessary noise is stealing your right to quiet. The .58% per decibel property value-noise relationship multiplier could be used to calculate the exact percentage of reduction for properties experiencing noise nuisance above the 60 decibel level.

For instance, if your property is located close to a major highway and you hear the road traffic from your front door registering 70 decibels, that diminishes the marketability of your property by 5.8% (number of decibels, in this example, 10 decibels x 0.58%) when compared to similar properties that do not suffer this detriment.

Studies show that every extra car added to street traffic has a corresponding negative effect on single-family housing prices.[56] The least expensive Sound Level Meters have a self-contained microphone, accuracy of +(-) 3 dB with scales 35 dB-100 dB and sell for $135.00 in the Grainger catalog (toll-free order # 1-800-323-0620).

77

Smoke, Odors: Exhaust fumes from rush-hour traffic may lead to carbon monoxide poisoning. Carbon monoxide is inhaled replacing oxygen and adheres to the hemoglobin in the blood and thereby reduces the amount of oxygen to body cells. Headaches, dizziness, drowsiness, confusion and cherry pink skin are some of the symptoms of carbon monoxide poisoning.

Air pollution from acid aerosols and soot poses a "deadly public health threat" to 23 million Americans (9.1% of the country's population) according to the American Lung Association.[56] These pollutants (called particulates) turn the air chalky or hazy and are more visible in the summer months.

The EPA standard for particulates (only those small enough to be inhaled) is 150 micrograms per cubic meter of air. Some sources of air pollution are: excessive factory smoke, utility smokestacks, wood burning, mining operations, diesel bus and truck emissions as well as car exhaust. Chronic respiratory illness, such as asthma, bronchitis, and emphysema can result from constant exposure to particulate air pollution.

If your comparables suffer equally from a shared determent, the sale prices of your comparables already reflect any adjustment. However, point out this off-site influence as having an overall depressing market effect compared to unplagued locations. If you live on a busy main street, busy corner lot or are exposed to particulate pollution, you have cause for an adjustment. Traffic levels are inversely related to single-family housing prices.

Bad industrial odors affect the sellability of one's home. If you are located next to a landfill, transfer station or a bad smelling industrial site, that may diminish your marketability by 10% or more. A neighborhood fish market, dry cleaner, livestock, etc. could be another plight requiring adjustment.

VIEW

Two comparisons are required:

1. Indicate either "Good," "Average," "Fair" or "Poor" for view.

2. Rate the comparables as "Superior," "Equal" or "Inferior" as compared to your property.

The view is considered to be what is seen from the inside of the house looking out. A property with a view of mountains, valleys, lakes or the seashore is more valuable than one that has no view. For example, if your house is in sight of a waste facility, cemetery, or is blocked from a view by high buildings, signs, etc. you have reason for an adjustment.

If you live in a built-up area and have surrounded your property with a walled area and/or created garden-type areas seen from your home's interior, and your comparable does not have such a view, the comparable would be adjusted higher. Multiple regression analysis conducted in Fairfax County, Virginia, proved an 8% addition to value for a single-family house with a good view. Real estate agents erroneously said that a good view was worth anywhere from 0-15% in the same market area tested.[57]

So what is a view worth? Found this in the Desert Morning News from Utah, dated 11/27/05: the Lake County section of Suncrest has the highest property taxes in Utah this year: $1,979 on a $200,000 home. Unincorporated Wayne County, where the subject homeowner of this report lives near Bicknell, has the lowest: $880 on a $200,000 home.

That is a $1,099 additional property tax for a view on a same-value home. View levels in Utah vary and fluctuate a lot. What we see here is this particular property tax assessor valued a good view upward at 54%!!

If you have a question as to what a buyer would pay for a specific view, ask a few Realtors® or appraisers for their opinion. The most accurate method to arrive at the value of the view is to use <u>matched pairs</u>. Find a sale(s) of nearly identical property with similar view(s) compared to sales of equally identical properties without a view. After adjusting for minor differences between the properties, their difference is the adjustment.

DESIGN AND APPEAL

Two comparisons are required:

1. Indicate building design for the subject and show appeal as "Good," "Average," "Fair" or "Poor."

2. Rate the comparable against the subject as either "Superior," "Equal" or "Inferior."

DESIGN: Try to find comparables that are of the same building design as yours. This may not always be possible. Some examples of home design are: Split Level, Split Entry, Bi-Level, Raised Ranch, Ranch, one-and-a-half-story Cape Cod, Early English, Tudor, Victorian, New England Colonial, Monterey, Italian, Spanish, or French Provincial, Georgian, Southern Colonial, Dutch Colonial or Contemporary.

It may be difficult to find recently sold homes similar to your home's design to use as comparables. Use the nearest type of design similar to yours that also has a similar room count and similar square footage.

This category of design and appeal is a measure of architectural attractiveness, which should be similar to your house. Public opinion dictates style and design for a given period in time. If prospective home buyers do not like the design or style of a house, then its value drops. Tract houses built right after World War II are often adjusted for poor design.

House Size Design Categories

One-story house: This is often referred to as a ranch and has all living area confined to one level. It does not have stairs unless it is to the basement. It is easy to maintain and usually has a low-pitched roof.

One-and-a-half-story house: This is called a Cape Cod, with usually half the attic space having headroom to be used as living space. It has a low price/gross living area and is easy to expand.

Two-story house: This design features one foundation and one roof serving twice as much floor area, lower cost for plumbing, electrical, heat and air conditioning systems since systems line up easier and can be stubbed off more economically, conserves on heating and cooling fuel bills.

Two-and-a-half-story house and *Three-story or more house:* These designs can be described as large New England Colonial, Southern Colonial and Tudor-style homes (among others). The cost of constructing additional square footage would be more economical than for a two-story.

"Split level": This adapts to a moderately sloping lot, has an entry between two floors, and has 3 or more separate levels of living space.

"Split entry": Sometimes called a raised ranch, split entry or split foyer, this is a one-story house raised a half-story above the ground which gives the basement area light and is often used for rec. rooms, etc.

APPEAL: Some houses' appeal are inappropriate for their property locations. A large 3,000-foot contemporary house would be out of place on a 50 by 100 foot lot. Many older subdivisions appear to be crowded by having too large a house on a small property. Buildings normally cover one-half of the lot in residential neighborhoods.

An 80:20 building-to-land ratio would probably reduce the value of the property.[58] Appeal considers the overall impression in terms of design, livability, age, condition and general features as it would appeal to an average home buyer. Renovation work that is out of character with the rest of the house will suffer market resistance.

An example of a feature that should be adjusted to reflect a greater appeal is a southern exposure. Experienced home buyers prefer homes with southern exposures. These houses often incorporate large overhangs to reduce exposure to the summer sun and will still allow ample sun in the winter months.

Design and appeal is an overall impression rating. Choose comparables similar to yours. Without genuine matched-pair evidence, obtaining a reliable adjustment should take into account the reproduction cost new and subtract for depreciation.

Other House Description Categories

Condominiums: Owner has a deed for unit, has a separate mortgage, pays property tax on the unit plus a percentage of the common areas and pays a monthly maintenance fee. A board of directors governs the complex with each owner having one vote. The condominium owner has a fee simple absolute unrestricted ownership and is individually responsible for property taxes and maintenance fees.

Use the sales price of condominiums with similar size, appeal, age, neighborhood, incurring similar maintenance fees, etc. to determine market value.

Cooperatives: Most co-ops are incorporated and a board of directors governs the complex with the owner of each individual unit having one vote. The owner has no deed, only stock and a proprietary lease which has a term from 10-50 years renewable automatically or at the discretion of the shareholders. He/she cannot refinance his unit as a condo owner can. "Mortgage, property tax and maintenance fees are paid pro rata by the owner according to the percentage of the overall size of the unit."[59] Property tax appeals involve the corporation and the stockholders.

Manufactured Homes: If it was built under the Federal Home Construction and Safety Standards established by HUD in June 1976, little if any valuation difference exists between manufactured homes and conventionally-built homes. Prefabricated, modular, or sectional housing should look like site-built houses to meet local building codes. There is very little difference in style, design or size; however, there may be quality differences.

Use similarly manufactured home sales for comparables if they are available. Usually that's impossible and regular stick built home must be used. You may be able to detect a buyer preference for site-built homes and use this as a favorable adjustment factor.

Mobile Homes: They account for almost 10% of existing single-family homes in the United States. Surveys show that mobile homes are not moved when they are sold in place and they are affected by the same influences as the conventional housing market. Book values from a reference guide are extremely inconsistent with the market. They do not accurately reflect market value due to lack of available park space.

Use the residential market approach as it is more realistic for determining value. Include resale's from other parks as long as the amenities are similar to the subject park. Note if it is on a permanent foundation, if it is set on piers and posts or if there are park premiums. Also include a full-cost approach from a mobile home trade publication (see Appendix), and note if it is built under HUD standards.

Residential Airparks: This home is located in an airport with an attached hanger and taxiway access to the runway. Homes in the growing 400+ residential airparks vary in price and appeal. Adjust for amenities. Use similar comparables as available.

Waterfront Houses: The value of a waterfront home is greatly influenced by the location, view, size and shape, water acidity (important for fish yield and abundance of underwater vegetation), depth, clarity, and type of shoreline. Use comparable sales from the same body of water that are most similar to the subject's situation. See page under "Site" for a closer examination.

Shore Homes: The value of a shore home is greatly influenced by the width of the beach, the view of the beach, the distance to the beach or if it is low-lying and subject to storm surge. If located directly on the beach, beach frontage footage increases value. See page under "Site" for closer examination.

Log Homes: Log homes are becoming more popular especially in rural areas. There is very little difference in the replacement or reproduction cost of log homes compared to conventional framed homes. In areas where there is not an ample supply of log homes, use similar size and types of residential property as comparables.

Historical Homes: These are difficult to ascribe a value to and in the end, the process of valuation may be better described as an art than a science. Identifying the historical value hinges on historical significance, identification with historical personages and events, architectural values, suitability and cost of restoration and maintenance, educational value, etc. Multiplication factors of 100-300% that of the non-historical valuation are not uncommon. The valuation of historic homes is a specialized field in itself and is beyond the scope of this book.

QUALITY OF CONSTRUCTION

Two comparisons are required:

1. Enter quality of construction rating as "Low," "Fair," "Average," "Good," "Very Good" and "Excellent."

2. Give an overall rating for the subject property and give a comparable evaluation for each of the comparables indicating if "Superior," "Inferior" or "Equal."

Low Quality: This classification of building is built with low-quality materials and workmanship. Foundation on

85

masonry piers, wood posts or foundation not below the frost line, poor quality spackling and/or partitions, soft wood floors and trim although occasionally a poor-quality hardwood floor is found. Electric heat and/or wood stove. The plumbing usually consists of a three-fixture bath and kitchen sink.

Fair Quality: Foundation is 8 inches poured concrete below the frost line, 8 inches concrete block foundation and may have a poor stucco finish. Usually found with adequate electrical, heating and plumbing facilities, but fixtures are less than average quality. Partitions of plaster or drywall, floor and roof framing may be less than standard. It has all the essentials, but most materials and workmanship are slightly inferior in quality.

Average Quality: This building is usually built by developers on a mass production basis. Materials, fixtures and workmanship are of average quality meeting the minimum building code standards. Rafters, floor joist and framing are according to standard size and spacing. Plumbing facilities usually consist of a three-fixture bath, kitchen sink, water heater and laundry facilities. Stock kitchen cabinets.

Good Quality: This building is usually built to individual specifications with a greater emphasis on architecture, with materials, fixtures and workmanship showing good quality. Floor joists and rafters are better than average size, trim and doors usually of hardwood, expensive plumbing and heating system but not the highest quality available. Ample kitchen cabinets with built-in ovens, garbage disposal, dishwasher, etc.

Very Good Quality: This building has the highest architectural treatment, best grade of construction materials, fixtures and best craftsmanship available. It has the finest grade of plumbing, most expensive fixtures, custom-designed kitchen, a finer grade of cabinet work and trim and a high quality of roof covering.

Excellent: Mansions. This is a specialized field and beyond the scope of this book.

The quality of the living space is often more valued than the quantity of the living space. Physical attributes like vaulted ceilings, architectural smoothness, efficient use of space, quality of materials used as well as intangibles, like positioning the house to a southern exposure or positioning the house in flow with the natural terrain, add qualitative differences. Some homes have a good layout (functional utility), however, the workmanship may be poor and/or the materials used may not be as good a quality as they could have been. On the other hand, a house may be overbuilt for the area in which it is situated. A knowledgeable purchaser would pay little extra for it.

Use houses of a similar quality of construction, since if it is not equivalent to your property, the quality of construction will be a major adjustment. The quality of construction in a particular builder's subdivision is typically the same. "When adequate documentation is provided to support the value difference estimate and the inability to use the paired sales extraction method, the cost calculation handbook quality comparison method may be used."[60] Use the cost new (cost information from Marshall & Swift Residential Cost Handbook), less depreciation from all causes (see Chapter 9) to arrive at a final valuation.

For instance, if you are comparing average quality one-story houses and the only difference in quality is the type of roof (your house has a composition shingle or built up, small rock roof as a base price), adjust comparables per square foot for a wood shingle roof at -$ .84, wood shake at -$ .99, concrete tile at -$1.70. Factor in local cost multipliers found in Marshall & Swift Residential Cost Handbook (See Appendix C for additional source reference.)

"You may delay, but time will not." - Benjamin Franklin

AGE

Enter the age of the house.

Indicate "Superior," "Equal" or "Inferior" if adjustment is entered.

Overall upkeep is important to the age of a house. Of older homes in good condition, an age difference of plus or minus five years generally will not affect the value of the comparable. In most subdivisions, there is no significant difference in the ages of residences since they are completed within a few years' time.

Usually, it is possible to determine when a house was built by lifting the lid on the water closet for the toilet and looking on the underside. The month, date and year of manufacture is impressed in the underside of the porcelain lid.

Look for similar age homes as comparables. If the year when a comparable house was built differs from your house, use an adjustment of about 1% of the selling price per year to reflect the difference.[61] For example, if the subject house is 7 years old and if Comparable #1 is new and sold for $225,000, take 7% from $225,000 or - $15,750 adjustment in the adjustment column to reflect the difference. (Look under "Age" in example #2 in Chapter 4.)

It is usually more economical to restore an older home than to build a new one thereby resulting in many quality restored older homes. However, when comparing older homes, it may be difficult to compare similar qualities the subject has such as electrical wiring, insulation, plumbing, etc. Therefore, the effective age of an older house is a more accurate estimation of age than the actual age. A lower effective age, when compared to a higher actual age, is a good indication of a home that is well maintained. A recently restored older home would have a very low effective age.

If you decide on using the effective age as a yardstick, enter **Effective** by the word age or if you are using both effective and actual, differentiate by indicating **A-30, E-25.** For a more detailed explanation of effective age, look under Depreciation in Chapter 9.

CONDITION

Two comparisons are required:

1. The condition of the subject property would be rated "Good," "Average," "Fair" or "Poor."

2. Rate the comparables as "Superior," "Equal" or "Inferior."

Normal maintenance and repairs do prevent property value from falling and do not warrant an increase in assessments. If someone allows their property to deteriorate, then the assessed value should decrease. An adjustment in this category would show that the comparable is in better or worse shape than yours. If you see that there is more than a 10% difference in the condition of your house compared to the comparable, find a comparable that is more similar.(62)

89

If there is a difference in condition due to physical factors, for example, it needs exterior paint, minor carpentry or a new roof, use the cost to do this work as an adjustment. Include a written addendum describing and clarifying the adjustment; for example, a new roof. So as not to duplicate "Age" in the "Condition" adjustment, use only curable conditions. The "Age" adjustment reflects only incurable conditions. Therefore, do not make an adjustment for replacing an element of the structure if it is still functioning well.(63)

Some defects are cosmetic in nature and may be ignored by the market while some defects substantially decrease the property's value. For instance, minor flaking and cracking of concrete may be acceptable, but improperly prepared footings caused by soft, untamped (not compressed) soil will settle causing foundations to crack requiring a large adjustment.

"Conditions which do not ordinarily require repair include any surface treatment, beautification or adornment which is not connected to work required for the preservation of the property, its continued physical soundness or marketability, or the health and safety of its occupants. Some examples are:

- A wood floor whose finish has been worn off to expose the bare wood must be sanded and refinished; however a wood floor which has darkened with age, but has an acceptable finish, does not need polishing or refinishing.
- Peeling interior paint and broken or seriously cracked plaster or sheetrock require repair and repainting; but paint which is adequate, though not fresh, need not be redone.
- Missing shrubbery or dead grass on an existing property need not be replaced.

- Cleaning or removal of carpets is required only when they are so badly soiled as to affect the livability and/or marketability of the property.
- Installation of paved driveways or aprons should not be required if an otherwise acceptable   surface is present.
- Installation of curbs, gutters or partial paving of a street is not required unless assessment for the same is imminent.
- Complete replacement of tile floors is not necessary if it is done because some of the original tiles do not match.
- Minimum amperage is 60-100 amps, but varies from region to region."[64] To estimate amperage capacity, count the number of circuit breakers or fuses.

> 30 Amp Service--4 breakers or fuses
> 60 Amp Service--6-8 breakers or fuses
> 100 Amp Service--10 to 16 breakers or fuses
> 150 Amp Service--20 or more breakers or fuses

A HUD requirement for existing housing is that natural ventilation of structural spaces such as attics and crawl spaces must be provided in order to reduce the effect of conditions of excess heat and moisture which are conducive to decay and deterioration of the structure.[65] A crawl space must have adequate distance (at least 18") between the floor joists and the ground, adequate ventilation and access (at least a 24" x 24" opening).

Another standard requirement for existing housing by HUD is that when re-roofing a defective roof already consisting of 2 layers of shingles, all old shingles must be removed prior to re-roofing.[66]

Check List of Repair Items

- Roof leaks and shingle replacement, flashing, gutters and/or down-spouts, fascia and/or soffit
- Siding repair, paint building, graffiti removal, caulking windows, glass and screen repair
- Moisture damage to exterior insulation and finish systems (EIFS). This is synthetic stucco applied over foam sheathing. 90% or more of randomly tested EIFS houses in North Carolina have some problem with damages averaging $3,000-$5,000 and many ranging $30,000-$100,000.(67)
- Repair to chimney(s), stucco, cement plastering, brick, block or stone repair
- Cracked sidewalk(s), cracked driveway and parking areas, garage door repair
- Minor carpentry, worn out counter tops, broken plaster or sheetrock, interior paint, wallpaper
- Loose, cracked or deteriorated floor tile, linoleum, carpet, ceramic tile, wood floors worn through the finish
- Damaged, inoperative or inadequate plumbing, heating or electrical systems, electrical repair, plumbing leaks, broken or missing fixtures
- Termite, ant or vermin extermination with attending structural repair costs
- Installation of safety handrails, fire alarms or correction of unsafe conditions required by law
- Dampness in basement
- Repair to septic system

Minor repair items usually add more value than their costs and a contractor's estimate for repairs would greatly substantiate the adjustment. If, in your judgment, the cost of the repairs adds nothing to the value of the property, then you should not look for an adjustment for that item. However, many neglected minor repairs become a substantial cause for a reduction in market value.

ABOVE GRADE ROOM COUNT

Enter total number of rooms.

"The key criterion for the comparison of single-family residences is the number of bedrooms. Regardless of the volume of space in a house, the number of bedrooms is the first element of similarity that should be used. In a market area there is a rather precise relationship between the number of baths or lavatories and the number of bedrooms."(68)

Total Rooms: The total number of rooms, excluding bathrooms, entry hall, small pantry and any basement (below grade) rooms is tabulated. This includes all bedrooms, living room(s), dining room(s), laundry or utility room, recreation room, library, den, large pantry room, music room, sewing room, etc.

The foyer (entrance to the house) is excluded from the room count. A dining room off the kitchen counts as an extra room if a hypothetical wall could be inserted to separate the two areas. Also, if either room can be used without inconvenience and the rooms are characteristic of other dining rooms in the market, they are considered separate rooms.(69)

Garages are never tallied, porches are tallied only if heated, habitable attics above 5 ft. in height are tallied if they are heated and finished like the rest of the house. Typically, appraisers will not make an adjustment for differences in room count or for differences in room square footage and, if they do so, an explanation should follow.(70)

Total Bedroom(s): Tally all bedrooms for bedroom room count.

Total Bath(s): Full bath (toilet, sink, and tub and/or shower) and half-baths (toilet and sink) are tallied. Some areas count 4 fixtures as a bath (toilet, sink, tub and shower) and 3 fixtures as 3/4 bath. A quarter bath consists of 1 fixture (a toilet only).

A room with only a basin or only a shower would be listed under the last category, "Other." Average quality full-bath adjustments generally range from $3,000-$5,000, half-baths range from $1,000-$2,500.

Note: The only adjustments entered for this category are for differences in the number of bathrooms. Differences in room count are reflected in the total dollar per square footage adjustment in the following gross living area category.

GROSS LIVING AREA:

Enter square footage of living space.

To determine the total square footage of your house, use only outside measurements since that is the standard used. Be sure to include only living space, not garages, Florida rooms, work-shops or other typically unheated and/or not air-conditioned areas, in these calculations. Measure around the outside of the house for each level above the foundation. Do not include the basement even if it is finished and heated unless it is 100% above grade.

Porches are included only if they are finished and heated and similar in appearance to the rest of the house. Garages are never included. Include habitable attics that have normal ceiling heights equivalent to the rest of the house.

Square footage information on comparables will most likely be found in MLS "sold" books. If you have difficulty determining the square footage of your comparable(s), you may have to estimate the square footage. The dimensions of the rooms are usually given in the MLS data; add 20-25% to the total room square footage to account for hallways and closets for a typical house.

Since this figure varies according to the style of the house that you are comparing, for greater accuracy you can determine the percentage of your own house's square feet that is composed of hallways and closet space and use that percentage with similar style comparable(s).

However, in the interest of incontestability, one can ask permission of the new owner to measure the perimeter of his house. As an incentive, you can offer to share the results of your appeal. Be aware that with the Multiple Listing Service comparables there is a small probability of error in square foot calculation because of faulty measurements or an error in transcription. It would show up where square footage does not add up to the individual calculations under "Room" description in the "Property Description" for the sold property.

The following method must be used to adjust for size differences in order to account for square foot differences between comparables:[71]

Gross Price Per Square Foot and House to Land Valuation Ratio

The Current Assessed Value - The Assessed Improved Value = The Assessed Land Value

For instance, in a neighborhood of million dollar homes, if the current assessed value for the subject property is $1,000,000 and the assessed improved value is $600,000, than the assessed land value is $400,000. The subject home in this example has 5,000 square feet.

40% of the value for the current assessed value for the property is in the land.

Here we are trying to estimate the gross square foot living space for a comparable. <u>Since it is in the same neighborhood as the subject property, we assume the same house/land valuation ratio of 40%.</u>

We learn that Comparable A sold for $8,000,000 and has 4,000 square feet. It is 1,000 square feet smaller than the subject property.

$800,000 divided by 4,000 square feet = $200 per square foot. But since we determined that 40% of that value is found in the land and 60% in the building, the actual square footage multiplier value is $120 per square foot (.60 x $200).

The difference in square footage adjustment against the subject home: 1,000 sq. ft. x $120 per square foot equals an $120,000 adjustment basis. This is a positive (+) adjustment in order to make that item equal to that in the subject property. Or in other words, if a comparable sale property has a major fault that your property does not have, a positive adjustment is required to make the comparable property equal to the subject property.

Subject	Comparable A
Gross Living Area: 5,000 sq. ft.	4,000 sq. ft.
Adjusted Sales Price of Comp:	<u>$800,000</u>
Adjusted Final Value:	$920,000

From this one comparable example we see that the subject property is worth less than the $1,000,000 assessment because of the gross square foot adjustment.

To make your case for any overall value conclusion, you'll need 3 comparables.

(1) Subtract the site value from the sales price of the comparable.

To ascertain the site value find the assessments in the neighborhood off the tax assessor's public record. This house-to-land relationship can be quite varied. It can be less than 20% and greater than 50%, but usually it is in the 20% - 25% value range. Check the land/building ratio by dividing the land value by the building value from data of similar area homes in the tax assessment record. See Chapter 4, example #2 and example #4 for a representative complete application.

If the comparable has a garage, carport, basement, tennis court, etc., subtract the estimated value of those features.

(2) Divide the remaining amount in item (1) by the total square feet of living area in the comparable to obtain the sale price per square foot of living area.

(3) Subtract the total square feet of living area in the comparable from the total square feet of living area in the subject. When the comparable dwelling has more living area than the subject, the answer will be negative (-).

(4) Multiply the square foot difference by the price per square foot obtained from the calculation in item (2). The answer will be the amount of dollar adjustment to make to the comparable to compensate for the amount of sale price contributed to the difference in size.

When the size difference is a negative amount (smaller than what it is being compared to), the adjustment to the comparable will be a negative adjustment. Adjustments for value differences caused by site, garage and/or carport differences will be made later (adjusted in specific categories found within the Residential Market Analysis form).

The following examples illustrate this method of estimating value differences due to the size of living area:

Assume Comparable A sold for $40,000 and had a single-car garage valued at $3,000 and a site value of $8,000. The dwelling contained 1,200 square feet of living area. Assume the subject property has 1,100 square feet of living area. The following calculations are made:

$40,000 - $3,000 - $8,000 = $29,000 net dollar amount of living area for Comparable A.

$29,000 ÷ 1,200 sq. ft. = $24.17 per square foot of living area for Comparable A.

1,100 sq. ft. -1,200 sq. ft. = -100 sq. feet difference between subject and Comparable A.

-100 sq. ft. x $24.17 = -$2,417 adjustment to the comparable for size difference (rounded off equals a minus $2,400 adjustment).

Comparable B sold for $49,000, had a site value of $5,000, a double-car garage valued at $4,000, and a basement valued at $10,000. The dwelling had 1,000 square feet of living area. Assume the subject has 1,100 square feet of living area. The following calculations are made:

$49,000 - $5,000 - $4,000 - $10,000 = $30,000 net dollar amount of living area for Comparable B.

$30,000 ÷ 1,000 sq. ft. = $30.00 per square foot of living area for Comparable B.

1,100 sq. ft. - 1,000 sq. ft. = +100 square foot difference between subject and Comparable B.

+100 sq. ft. x $30.00 = +$3,000 adjustment to the comparable for size difference.

If there is a 5% or less difference in square footage, no adjustment is necessary.[72] Nevertheless, every adjustment in your favor should be taken.

BASEMENT AND FINISHED ROOMS BELOW GRADE

Two comparisons are required:

1. Note the type of improvement in the basement (e.g. bedroom, rec. room, laundry) and if the basement is "Full" or "Partial," "Finished" or "Unfinished" or "None."

2. Indicate if comparables are "Superior," "Inferior" or "Equal." If there is/are finished room(s) below grade, indicate room types (e.g. Bdrm, Den, Rec Rm, etc.).

A crawl space is not a basement. According to The Federal National Mortgage Association (Fannie Mae), a basement is considered to be any part of a building area that is below grade (grade means the same level as the ground). "Only finished above-grade areas should be used. Garages and basements (including those that are partially above-grade) should not be included.

We consider a level to be below-grade if any portion of it is below-grade regardless of the quality of its 'finish' or the window area of any room. Therefore, a walk-out basement with finished rooms would not be included in the above-grade room count."(73) A below-grade room is a basement room; therefore a bathroom below-grade is not included in the room count. Although rooms in raised ranch, bi-level and split level homes that are below grade are usually counted as above-grade rooms by appraisers, these rooms should be considered basement rooms according to Fannie Mae's strict guidelines. Make appropriate entries and adjustments for finished rooms in this section. Fannie Mae's guidelines are important because they've become the standard for the appraisal industry.

Because the basement cost more to build does not necessarily mean that a buyer in the market will pay extra for it. In regions where basements are expected, a house without a basement is at a disadvantage. In some areas where most of the houses are built on a slab, basements may be of little value.

Climatic conditions also play a central role in determining the value or lack of value of having a basement. Basements are found in most homes in Northern and Midwestern states and more rarely in Southern and Southwestern regions. The amount of adjustment for a basement in California may be small in relationship to its cost. On the other hand, a house without a basement in Massachusetts may require a large adjustment close to the cost of a new basement since basements are normal in that area.

Typical adjustments for average-quality finished basements may range from $3,000 to $12,000+; an unfinished basement may range from $1,000 to $5,000+. An outside basement entrance can improve the basement by $700 to $2,000. A house with a basement verses a house without a basement is typically valued at $5 per square foot by appraisers. Reproduction cost for a new basement is $15 per square foot and an argument can be made to use this figure considering structural components depreciate very little.

FUNCTIONAL UTILITY

Two comparisons are required:

1. Rate the subject as: "Good," "Average," "Fair" or "Poor."
2. Enter rating for comparables as: "Superior," "Equal" or "Inferior."

This is the area to deduct for instances of deficiencies or over-built features. Deficiencies include items such as:

- Poor floor plan.
- Front entrance opens directly into the living room.
- Rooms are badly proportioned.
- Inefficient counter space or lack of kitchen cabinets.
- Kitchen on a different level from the dining room
- House hard to heat or ventilate.
- Bedroom with entrance through another bedroom.
- Bedroom(s) and bath visible from living room or entrance.
- Bedroom(s) on a level with no bath.
- Awkward arrangement of rooms.
- Inadequate storage space for clothes, linens, supplies and maintenance tools.
- Halls too narrow.

- House has very low ceilings.
- Inappropriate location of stairway
- Narrow width and steepness of stairs and/or threads and risers inappropriate.
- Unacceptable door size through which to move furniture.
- Wall between bedrooms not soundproof (or not soundproofed by adjacent bath or closet).
- No outside access to basement.
- Poor location of family room.
- Rooms too small.
- Excessive size of rooms.
- Undesirable site design regarding relationship of retaining walls, walks, driveway and outside landscaping, etc.

Some of these conditions are incurable; other conditions are curable. Examples of curable conditions are: remodernizing a kitchen, installing an adequate new heating system, upgrading an electrical service, etc. When entering an adjustment for a curable condition, the cost to cure must be less than the total remodeling or rehabilitating cost.

For example, most home buyers prefer a second bathroom in a 3+ bedroom house. To include an extra bathroom in the new construction plans costs $7,000. If remodeling expenses were $10,000 to convert space in order to furnish this bath, the functional utility lost by not having this bath is $3,000. Unplanned expenses for providing plumbing, electrical and heating connections constitute the majority of this adjustment.

In some cases the cost of the structure is much more than its market value and an adjustment needs to be made for an over-improvement or a non-essential luxury. A swimming pool, greenhouse, extra large room(s), over-enhanced kitchen, over-built patio or deck, tennis court, superior grade fixtures, etc. are not as valuable to the eyes of a typical buyer in the market when compared to their reproduction cost.

Many built-in appliances use 220-240 volt service and a service of greater strength (measured in amperage) is needed. The circuit breaker or fuse panel should be at least 100 amps. A 150-200 amp service may be required in a larger house with electric heat, however with conventional heat this extra capacity could be viewed as an over-improvement.

FHA minimum standards for room size serve as a guide which must be modified for the different qualities of constructed homes. If a room size is less than the market expectation, a justification for loss due to lack of functional utility is confirmed. For higher quality homes, these standards are not desired and have little relevance. Room sizes for individual sold homes are recorded in MLS Books.

FHA Minimum Standards for Room Size:

Living Room	11' x 15'6" (170 sq. ft.)
Galley Kitchen	10' x 8' (80 sq. ft.)
Standard Kitchen	10' x 10' (100 sq. ft.)
Dining Room	8'4" x 12' (100 sq. ft.)
Master Bedroom	9'.4" x 13' (120 sq. ft
Bedroom (twin bed)	11'6" x 12' (138 sq. ft.)
Bedroom (double bed)	10' x 11'6" (115 sq. ft.)
Bathroom	5' x 7' (35 sq. ft.)
Lavatory	4' x 5' (20 sq. ft.)

HEATING/COOLING

Note the type of heating and cooling.

Heating systems typically include oil or gas-fueled forced warm air, hot water radiation, steam heat system, electric hot air or hot water systems, heat pumps, and passive or active solar heat systems.

Moveable window air conditioner units are not a permanent part of the house and therefore no adjustment is made for them. Central air conditioning is considered a permanent part of a structure, therefore, make adjustments for the presence or lack of this feature. Heat pumps (acting like a reversible refrigeration unit) used to both heat or cool a house are another positive feature.

Adjustments reflect the absence or presence of air conditioning or the type, condition and effectiveness of the heating equipment. For example, an electric baseboard heating system in a colder northern climate would be more expensive to operate than a conventional hot water baseboard system and could have a $4,500 or more adjustment.

In western or southern climates, central air conditioning is standard and the unit plus the cost of installation (about $4,000) can be used as an adjustment. In cooler climates, central air may be viewed as non-essential and a smaller adjustment would be in order.

SPECIAL ENERGY-EFFICIENT ITEMS

Two divisions of information require evaluation:

1. Enter type of improvement for subject and comparables.

2. Rate comparables as "Superior," "Equal" or "Inferior."

Note if there are storm windows, replacement windows, double or triple-pane thermopane windows (with or without high performance insulated glass). Note if there is a high-energy efficiency rating because of high R insulation (a measurement of resistance to heat flow; the higher the R factor, the greater its insulating properties) in ceilings and roofs, which should have an R rating of R-20 to R-24 (6 1/2" of fiberglass) or higher in cold climates (R-13 sufficient in mild climates).

Exterior walls should have an R rating of R-8 to R-12 (3 1/2" of fiberglass), floors should be at least R-9. Foundation walls commonly use ridged Styrofoam board with R ratings of R-12 or better. A water heater should have 3 inches of insulation with an R value of 12, and heating/cooling ducts and pipes commonly have 1" of insulation with an R rating of R-3 or better.

Meeting standard insulation expectations is not a reason for a special energy-efficient adjustment; superior insulation is. R-18 is twice as energy efficient as R-9. Also note solar heating units, ceiling fans, automatic setback thermostats, special solar window shades or blinds, window quilts, roof overhang intended for solar control in conjunction with southern exposure, or other energy conservation features.

Inches of Insulation Required

R-Value	BLANKETS	BLANKETS	LOOSE FILL
	Fiberglass	Fiberglass	Cellulite
R-11	3.5-4	5	3
R-13	4	6	3.5
R-19	6-6.5	8-9	5
R-22	6.5	10	6
R-26	8	12	7-7.5
R-30	9.5-10.5	13-14	8

SOURCE: U.S. Department of Energy

New efficient heating and cooling systems include such things as a high efficiency oil or gas furnace with an Annual Fuel Utilization Efficiency (AFUE) rating of 80% or higher, a high efficiency heat pump with a Seasonal Energy Efficiency Ration (SEER) measure of 9.0 or greater and a Heating Seasonal Performance Factor (HSPF) of 7.0 or greater, and a central air conditioner with a SEER rating of 9.0 or greater. System modifications include such things as a flame retention oil burner, vent dampers in oil and gas furnaces, pilotless ignition for gas furnaces, and a secondary condensing exchanger for gas and oil furnaces.[74]

Lack of energy-efficient items increases the utility bill cost and the typical buyer will pay less for that home compared to a home with normal energy efficiency. One method for estimating the value difference of heating and cooling an energy-inefficient home is to arrange for a comparative energy audit. This is usually a free service provided by the local utility company or private contractor.

Assume, for instance, that you have documented that your house will pay $50 per month extra in utility bills as compared to an energy-efficient house. Also assume that the property in question has a 30-year mortgage at 10% interest at the time of the market analysis. The amortized table (available at any library, bank, real estate or financial institution) indicates a $8.63 monthly payment on a $1,000 mortgage for 30 years at 10% interest (modify to meet prevailing loan market interest rate).

$8.63 per $1,000 = .00863 per $1.00

$50.00 ÷ .00863 = $5,793.74 ($5,800 rounded off)

This example shows that the purchaser could pay $5,800 more for an energy-efficient home and would have the same total monthly cost for loan payments and utilities. Therefore, this indicates that dwellings that are not energy efficient would be worth $5,800 less than the energy-efficient dwelling due to the lack of energy-efficient items.[75]

Again, there may be a difference in what an item costs and the value the market perceives the item is worth when regarding new-fangled energy-efficient items. Market value always prevails. When the R values (a measure of resistance to heat flow) are enlarged and equal reduction of utility bills is not matched, a point of diminishing returns is reached.

GARAGE/CARPORT

Two categories of information require evaluation:

1. Enter number of garages or "None."

2. Indicate if the comparables are "Superior," "Equal" or "Inferior."

Note if your property and comparable properties have garages or carports. In some areas, carports are the norm and a garage would constitute an over adequacy. Garages in these areas are considered an over-improvement and are valued less than areas where garages are common.

This same reasoning applies to an area where one or two-car garages are normal; in such an area a three-car garage would be considered an over-improvement and a carport would be a deficiency. The minimum standard size for a garage is 10 feet by 20 feet; 18.5 feet by 20 feet for a two-car garage. Adjustments are made on the basis of size, number and type of construction.

If a garage has been converted into a bedroom, den, family room, etc., and it has not been done in compliance with local building requirements, then a downward adjustment may be made for the cost of converting it back into its legal use as a garage (re-installing garage door and minor carpentry work).

If the conversion has been done with required building permits and if it is consistent with the rest of the house, then the full value as living area may be applied.(76) Garages that have been converted should be looked at for their functional utility. Was the extension of a heating system completed? Are there adequate electrical outlets?

Using the matched pair method, house A is very similar to house B, except that it has a three-car garage whereas house B does not. House A sold for $175,000 and house B sold for $165,500. Because the only difference between these two houses is that one has a garage and the other doesn't, the value of the garage is the difference in the sales price. The value of the garage in this example is $9,500.

Although the total cost may vary greatly, building a garage detached from the house will generally cost at least $45 per square foot. Valuation for garages or carports is based on the number of cars it will accommodate and if it is an *attached* (shares one or more common walls with the house), *detached* (shares no walls or ceilings) or *built-in* structure (shares one or more common walls with the house and the ceiling of the garage is the floor of the house). A high end garage with tile floor, finished walls and ceilings and depending on the type of construction and finish, could add considerably more value (see Marshall & Swift).

A detached garage generally adds 25% more value and a built-in garage subtracts about 35% from the above *attached* value range calculations. If you have a four-car garage and the neighborhood you live in has largely 1-2 car garages, the market value for the additional garage space will be marginal (the market value of the additional garages may only gain a marginal amount regardless of the additional building costs). If the garage or portion of the garage is an over-improvement, address only the contributory value of the over-improvement in your adjustment valuation.

PORCHES, PATIO, DECK, FIREPLACE(S), ETC.

Two divisions of information require evaluation:

1. List type of improvement.

2. Show relationship: "Superior," "Equal" or "Inferior."

109

Note any porch, patio, Florida room, pool, workshop, guest house or any living or recreation area not part of the primary house. If the comparable sale property unarguably has a major improvement and yours does not, make a minus adjustment. Conversely, if you enjoy a major improvement and the sale comparable does not, make a positive adjustment.

Be aware, when making adjustments to your comparables, of relational degrees of improvement. A deck, for example, can vary in size and complexity (multi-level deck, built-ins, bar-b-que pit, etc.). Note the number of fireplaces or wood-burning stoves. The value of the adjustment depends on the quality of the fireplace, if it is a one or two-story chimney, if it has special facing materials, etc.

In average-quality homes a screened porch may be typically valued at $20 per square foot by appraisers, patio $1,600-$3,500, typical deck adjustments $4,000-$7,500, fireplaces range $3,500-$12,000 (depending on the quality of the fireplace, one-or two-story chimney or special feature), wood-burning stoves range from $800-$1,500. It may be beneficial to call an appraiser, real estate agent or tax assessor for acceptable values in your area.

FENCE, POOL, ETC.

Two divisions of information require attention:

1. List type of improvement.

2. Show relationship: "Superior," "Equal" or "Inferior."

This category is used for improvements such as fences, retaining walls, driveways, landscaping, greenhouses, tennis courts, bomb shelters, etc.

Fences consist of a variety of materials, designs, and cost ranges. The height of the fence, quality of material, gauge of wire, metal inserts, etc., may add to the cost of the fence, however, the market appeal of this type of improvement may add little or no value to the property.

If your house has a pool and many of the neighbors have pools, then that is normal for your area. If none of the neighbors have pools and you have a pool, then you have an over-improvement. Different neighborhoods have different markets. A pool that cost $40,000 to build may add only $12,000 in value to a $200,000 house, but that same pool may add $40,000 in value to a $500,000 home in another neighborhood.

Without genuine matched-pair evidence, obtaining a reliable adjustment should take into consideration the reproduction cost new, subtracting physical depreciation (see Chapter 9) and then multiplying that figure by a percentage for functional loss. For instance, a swimming pool new costs $40,000 with a 20 year life. It is 10 years old. This gives us a $20,000 (depreciated amount) multiplied by 50% (estimated functional loss due to lack of buyers) resulting in a final valuation estimate of $10,000 for the swimming pool.

OTHER

Two categories require evaluation:

1. Enter type of improvement that would either add or subtract from value.

2. Show relationship: "Superior," "Equal" or "Inferior."

This section is a "catch all" for any unaddressed item(s) to which the market (the typical buyer) reacts. For example: newly remodeled kitchen, kitchen counters & cabinets and built-ins, walk-in pantry, bedroom walk-in closet, intercom system, remodeling, interior improvements, attic finish, vaulted ceilings, real wood paneling, unfinished rooms, fire and burglar alarm systems, water supply problems, plumbing system features or deficiencies, lavatory, electrical deficiencies or features, waste disposal system, indoor sauna, automatic sprinkler system, etc.

A recently remodeled kitchen that costs $15,000 may add only $9,300 to the value of the house. Kitchen equipment and new appliances included in the sale of the comparable (not classified as personal property of the seller), such as ranges, refrigerators, freezers, ovens, garbage compactors, disposals, dishwashers, etc. are additional grounds for an adjustment .

See: Cost vs. Value Report From Remodeling Magazine http://www.remodeling.hw.net

NET ADJUSTMENTS (TOTAL)

Total all adjustments and add to or subtract from the sales price of each comparable.

Total dollar amount of all adjustments for any given comparable, when compared to your house, should not exceed 25%. Any individual adjustment should be no greater than 15%.[77] The more the comparables are like your house, the less the adjustments will be, and the more accuracy will be increased. If these percentage limits are exceeded, comment on the reason for not using a more similar comparable.

Any category of the subject that is rated "less than average" ("fair" or "poor") should have an explanation. Also, it is worthwhile to include an addendum to underscore the credibility of deductions you are taking.

Include contractors' estimate(s), traffic studies backed by pictures (e.g. to show traffic congestion, etc.), data from a government study(s) or private study(s), a comparative analysis or any specific evidence that you feel will help your case.

As previously mentioned, all adjustments should reflect the market's reaction to the item adjusted for and what a typical buyer would pay. Do not completely rely on reproduction costs as an adjustment. Reproduction costs may serve as a guide and may be used to footnote an addendum, but should not be relied upon as a basis of valuation. Only the specific contribution or detraction to total market value should be counted.

ADJUSTED SALES PRICE OF COMPARABLES

Enter the total adjusted sales price of the three comparables. This total reflects all the additions and subtractions to the sales price of the comparable sales. These results are a direct estimated range of home values particular to the subject based on the residential market.

COMMENTS ON SALES COMPARISONS

Comment on why you have emphasized a particular comparable (similar in size, location, etc.).

For instance you may write at the bottom of the market analysis form, "Comparable sales are taken from nearby lakefront homes and are good indicators of market value. Greater emphasis was given to Comparable #1 because of similar size, date of sale and deep-water site location."

INDICATED VALUE OF SUBJECT

Enter the dollar amount of the indicated market value.

When finalizing your market value, the property that is most similar to the subject property should receive the most weight. However, if all things are equal, the comparable that was most recently sold should be stressed. This is not an averaging process, but rather a bracketing concept that assigns more emphasis to the comparable most similar to your property.

For example, Comparable #1 is most similar to your home and the values for Comparables #1, #2 and #3 are $200,000, $205,000 and $207,000 respectively. Double the value of the most similar property (Comparable #1) and add the remaining comparable values. Divide by 3. ($200,000 + $205,000 + $207,000 = $612,000 ÷ 3 = **$203,000**).

$103,000 becomes the finalized indicated value of the subject. Highlight this number with a fluorescent magic marker to leave a clear impression of the finalized valuation

COMMON OVERSIGHTS IN VALUATION

- Using comparables that are not comparable.
- Failure to indicate why subject and comparables are not located near each other.
- Failure to indicate how Gross Living Area was calculated and/or failure to calculate correctly.
- Failure to provide source reference for reproduction cost estimations.
- Failure to make an adjustment for personal property, such as kitchen equipment, with the comparables.

- Failure to use accurate, factual information.
- Failure to report how comparable sale information was verified; at least drive by them.
- Failure to show why comparable information more than 6 months old was used.
- Failure to justify or give adequate reasons for making large adjustments.
- Failure to explain the effects of detrimental influences to the value of the property.
- Failure to mention environmental problems often associated with older properties such as lead paint, asbestos-protected pipe insulation.
- Submitting poor photographs that fail to show subject and its surroundings.
- Mixing up the plus or minus adjustments.
- Math calculation errors.

Appeal, Quality of Construction, Age, Condition, and Functional Utility are all subjective factors that require subjective adjustments. Be careful that adjustments are reasonable and not excessive.

If a property is ever overvalued, a high probability exists that the reason can be traced to an excessive adjustment somewhere in this section. Adjustments should be made only in cases where the dissimilarity has a noticeable effect on the value. Small differences do not usually require adjustments."[78]

CHAPTER 4: GUIDELINES AND EXAMPLES OF MARKET ANALYSIS

"Diligence overcomes difficulties, sloth makes them." - Benjamin Franklin

EXAMPLES OF TYPICAL ADJUSTMENTS

Once you have selected the data that is particular to your comparable sales, you must organize and evaluate the information in order to reach a final value conclusion. In order to present this information in a universally accepted format, a standard reporting form is used. Forms, similar to the ones in this book, are used to evaluate information by real estate agents, appraisers, tax appeal attorneys, mortgage companies, insurance companies, government agencies, and other financial institutions.

Form reports began in the 1930's, but no standard type of reporting existed. Form standardization began in the 1970's and evolved up to 1986 when the Uniform Residential Appraisal Report (URAR) became the standard form. The updated June 1993 URAR form is the form of reference in our exhibit. We have adopted the analysis portion of this form, value conclusion section, photographic addendum, map location addenda, and additional information addenda.

The following five adjustment examples are for instructional purposes and allow you to follow the adjustment process. Normally, you would not use sales comparables that have the quantity of adjustments we have included. They are used merely to increase the variety of illustrations. To re-emphasize an earlier point, the less adjustments that are used, the more similar the comparison and the more accurate the indicated value of the subject.

As mentioned previously, if the comparable sale property has a major improvement and your property does not, make a minus adjustment. Conversely, if you enjoy a major improvement and the comparative sale property does not, make a positive adjustment.

NARRATIVE RESIDENTIAL MARKET ANALYSIS EXAMPLE #1

Since this is a larger graph than will fit with good visibility into this location, view this example http://propertytaxax.com/amazon/rma1.htm and follow the narrative explanation on that page.

NARRATIVE RESIDENTIAL MARKET ANALYSIS EXAMPLE #2

Since this is a larger graph than will fit in this location, view this example http://propertytaxax.com/amazon/rma2.htm and follow the narrative explanation on that page.

NARRATIVE RESIDENTIAL MARKET ANALYSIS EXAMPLE #3

Since this is a larger graph than will fit in this location, view this graph http://propertytaxax.com/amazon/rma3.htm and follow the narrative on that page.

NARRATIVE RESIDENTIAL MARKET ANALYSIS EXAMPLE #4

Since this is a larger graph than will fit in this location, view this graph http://propertytaxax.com/amazon/rma3.htm and follow the narrative explanation on that page.

NARRATIVE RESIDENTIAL MARKET ANALYSIS EXAMPLE #5

Since this is a larger graph than will fit in this location, view this graph http://propertytaxax.com/amazon/rma5.htm and follow the narrative explanation on that page.

CHAPTER 5: LAND VALUATION

"The wisdom of man never yet contrived a system of taxation that would operate with perfect equality." - Andrew Jackson

In most cases you need only be concerned with valuing your home. However, if you have a vacant piece of property and want to establish its true worth, the following chapter will help.

LAND VALUE

"Land," is classified in the language of the appraisers' world as: that portion of the earth's surface in its natural condition including trees, minerals, wildlife, water, as distinguished from "site," which is the land, its improvements and anything attached to it such as buildings, landscaping, fences, and any increase in utility from improvements such as roads, utilities, etc.

Perhaps the assessment on your building and improvements are justifiable, however, the land value portion of the assessment may be over valued. It may be beneficial to contest only the land value portion of the assessment. Every measure should be taken to gain an accurate value estimate. Comparisons should be consistent. A half-acre parcel should not be used as a comparison to a 10-acre parcel.

Explain and justify any adjustments for time, conditions of sale, location or physical distinctiveness. Give date of sale, price and method of verification of sales. A variety of land sale comparisons may be difficult to obtain in many suburbs or built-up areas, and it may be necessary to use more dated comparisons. Depending on the cycle in the real estate market, vacant land sales are usually more common in more rural areas.

SITE VALUE

Value difference may result due to lot size, shape, topography, and the view from the site; if it is surrounded by older homes, overlooking a nicely wooded area with a stream, next door to a service station on a heavily traveled street, located next to a railroad, etc. Adjustments must be made if the subject site has objectionable factors such as the lot being in a flood plain, seismic or mudslide area, and/or objectionable soil characteristics such as high shrink/swell potential if the comparable site did not have one or more of these objectionable features. See "Site" category for additional information.

Typical Characteristic Site Data

Area is one of the most important characteristics of a piece of land that affects its value. Zoning, deed restrictions, building code front, rear and side set-back restrictions may have a major effect on the property. 1 Acre = 43,560 sq. ft.

Frontage is the width of the front of a property which is parallel to the street and is normally expressed as "front feet." Refer to "4-3-2-1" land valuation on page 26.

Width in a regular lot is equivalent to the front feet. In an irregular lot, add the front and rear footage together and divide by two.

Depth is the distance from the front to the rear property line of a parcel (piece of land).

Shape may be regular, slightly irregular or very irregular and may have a direct bearing on its value.

Topography may determine the location of the building on the site and the type of construction.

Slope will determine what site improvement may be needed, such as retaining walls, drainage engineering and/or fill. Property is either level, downhill, uphill, side-hill, top-of-hill or bottom-of-hill. See slope table found in Index.

Drainage and Soil Conditions will determine if special footings are necessary. Bedrock will incur excess excavation cost.

Percolation is a test of the soil to determine its ability to absorb moisture. If a soil or site is determined to be poorly drained and has a corresponding high water table, it is unsuitable for construction.

View is more valuable if it is a good one; a poor view reduces value.

On-Site Improvements development costs such as clearing and grading, septic installation, well drilling, retaining walls, etc. increase site value. Review "Site" category.

Off-Site Improvements such as streets, sidewalks, electricity, water, gas, sewers, etc. greatly influence the value of the site.

Environmental Hazards such as excessive noise, high-tension towers, super-fund sites, toxic tailings from mining, radon, water quality, etc., greatly reduces the value of a site.

Location, as well as traffic noise and traffic hazards, have a significant influence on the value of property. See 'Location' on page 20-24, Chapter 3 for more details. If the land is rural, an estimate of added value should be made for fences, out-buildings, etc.

Easement or Encroachments or Zoning Restrictions need to be considered.

Reconciliation For The Assessment

If the sales ratio (also called average ratio, director's ratio, assessment level, the common level of 100% of true value, average percentage of full value, just valuation, the equalization rate, etc.) for the year is 91.2% then multiply this figure against the market value. Assume, for example, a $50,000 appraised value (true market value). To determine what the assessment should be, multiply $50,000 x .912 = $45,600.

Narrative Land Sales Comparison Example #1

Since this is a larger graph than will fit well here, view this graph http://propertytaxax.com/amazon/lsc1.htm and follow the narrative explanation on that page.

Narrative Land Sale Comparison Example #2

Since this is a larger graph than will fit in this location, view this graph http://propertytaxax.com/amazon/lsc2.htm and follow the narrative explanation on that page.

CHAPTER 6: GUIDELINES & AREAS FOR A TAX APPEAL

"When thou enter a city abide by its customs." - The Talmud

ARE YOUR PROPERTY TAXES WORTH APPEALING?

For example, the assessments are:

Current Assessed Land Value	$25,000
Current Assessed Improved Value	$193,000
Current Total Assessed Value	$218,000
Appraised Value as of 10/1/2012	$241,200
Sales Ratio (Director's Ratio, etc.)	71.7%
Suggested Total Assessed Value	**$172,940**

Suggested Assessed Value = Sales Ratio x Indicated Market Value (Appraised Value) **$172,940** = .717 x $241,200

Even though the assessed value is less than the fair market value, in this example, the assessment is quite out of line and substantial savings (21%) can be realized in appealing the old assessment. Remember: you are appealing your assessment, you are not appealing your taxes. Taxes are controlled by spending appropriations in your school district, spending appropriations championed by local politicians and their salary along with their "entitlement benefits packages." If you want to fight your taxes, you'll be in a different sort of battle trying to pry loose money that your representatives have claimed for themselves. In a tax appeal, <u>you are appealing *your assessment*</u>. You are seeking a current, equitable, fair, justifiable evaluation for your residence.

Divide the assessed value by the sales ratio to obtain the estimated value that the tax assessor says your house is worth. If your house is worth less, you may have a case worth pursuing.

Municipalities with 15% Range Requirements

In some municipalities, the assessed value is reduced only if it falls outside a 15% range of the sales ratio. This is sometimes called a Director's Ratio or Average Ratio. If the assessment falls within the range of the sales ratio, no adjustment will be made by the tax board. If you are appealing in the year of a revaluation or reassessment, the 15% range requirement will probably not be used since assessment and market value should be the same or very close together.

Using the so-called upper limit in your calculations will produce a figure below market value. This will reveal if your property assessment should be appealed.

EXAMPLE #1:

Assume we determine that the fair market value of our house to be $210,000.

Sales Ratio: = 99.2%
Common Level Ranges: .992 x .15 = .1488 or 14.88%

(mathematical note: when multiplying a percentage, move the decimal point 2 spaces to the left. To convert a decimal to a percentage, move the decimal point two spaces to the right.)
Add: 99.2% + 14.88% = 114.08% upper level (ratio must fall above this level to qualify)

Subtract: 99.2% - 14.88% = 84.32% lower level

Appraised Value (FMV)	= $210,000
Disputed Assessment	= $235,000
Judgment	**No Change in Assessment**

A $235,000 assessed value divided by the $210,000 appraised fair market value ($235,000 ÷ $210,000) = 111.9% ratio. This 111.9% ratio would not qualify for an adjustment since the suggested assessment falls within the director's ratio 15% range. If your ratio falls below the lower level, you should not appeal unless you want your taxes to increase!

Another way of looking at this using the assessment of $235,000 in our example and dividing it by the upper limit of 114.08%. (Mathematical note: when dividing by a percentage, don't forget to add two zeros to the result.) Answer: $205,815. This raises the question, is there something we overlooked, is the market value of our house below $205,815? If it is, we should appeal.

EXAMPLE #2:

Suppose we determine the fair market value of our house is $134,000.

Sales Ratio = 82.9%
Common Level Ranges: .829 x .15 = .1244 or 12.44%

(Mathematical note: when multiplying a percentage, move the decimal point 2 spaces to the left. To convert a decimal to a percentage, move the decimal point two spaces to the right.)

Add: 82.9% + 12.44% = 95.34% upper level (ratio must fall <u>above</u> this level to qualify)

Subtract: 82.9% - 12.44% = 70.46% lower level

Appraised Value (FMV)	= $134,000
Disputed Assessment	= $130,000
Judgment	**Change to Lower Assessment**

Using an entirely different sales ratio, in this example the $130,000 disputed assessment is divided by the $134,000 fair market value ($130,000 ÷ $134,000) resulting in a 97.0% ratio. This 97.0% ratio would qualify for an adjustment by the county tax board since the ratio falls <u>above</u> the sales ratio range. The Board of Adjustment should lower the assessment to $111,100 upon appeal by *multiplying* your fair market value of $134,000 by the sales ratio ($134,000 x .829 = $111,086).

Should we appeal our taxes? Similar to the previous example, using the assessment of $130,000 and dividing by the upper limit of 95.34% gives us a value of $136,354. (Mathematical note: when dividing by a percentage, don't forget to add two zeroes to the result.) If the market value of our house is below $136,354 we should appeal. In this example, we have determined the fair market value of our property is $134,000. Already we know we can save over 15% on our tax bill by appealing!

"If you carry your own lantern, you will endure the dark." - Hasidic saying

The MASS APPRAISAL PROCESS and PROPERTY RECORD CARDS

Mass Appraisal:

Mass appraisal is the process used by the local government for valuing a group of properties as of a given date. There are about 70,000 different taxing jurisdictions with different forms, deadlines and revaluation criteria to impose. For the taxing authority to employ an appraiser would be too costly. A mass appraisal is determined by legal and budgetary decisions.

The mass appraisal process provides valuation, although quickly obtained, on forms that become transferred to your property record card. To the person measuring your home, time is of the essence and errors occur. Sometimes the appraisal process involves merely driving by to note if there are any changes (windshield appraisal). Ask yourself, how much attention was given to your property if, perhaps, less than $15 was allocated per appraisal and the people employed to gather the information (hired by a mass appraisal contractor tying to make a profit) have questionable appraisal skills? Check for mechanical errors! Facts are often omitted, inaccurate data is often recorded! Property tax experts claim that 50% of homeowners may be paying more taxes than they should be due to <u>mistakes</u> in property assessments.[81]

In many states, residential property is paying a different percentage of market value than commercial property.

This is further complicated by various assessment ratios, the utilization of different approaches to value and bias exhibited in value ranges. Situations occur where lower-priced properties are not treated fairly compared with higher-priced properties.

Discrimination may occur due to age and location. Clusters of newer homes may be treated differently. Percentages of tax may vary on retail, multi-family, or commercial and industrial classifications. Property values for expensive residences and office buildings depreciate or appreciate at different rates (30% or greater depreciation has occurred since 2007 in many regions). Moderate-priced residential areas often pay a higher share for public services.

The economy achieved by mass appraisal verses the otherwise cost-prohibitive individual home appraisal system has certain built-in disadvantages. According to Mark Gardiner, the managing director of Public Financial Management Inc., a government financial advisory firm, "The closer you are to true market value, the better off you are. The farther you get away from 100% pure cash value, the more any mistake in assessment tends to be magnified."

To reiterate, because of the many restraints imposed by the mass appraisal process, inequities result. When properties are not reappraised on a regular basis, values get distorted resulting in comparable properties paying a significant difference in taxes.

"It is a national outrage that in an age of computer technology, most governments fail to administer property taxes fairly.... the average taxpayer in most states still is at the mercy of inexpert local officials, arbitrary bureaucracies and privileged interests. Antiquated administrative practices and insufficient

commitment of resources prevent even responsible officials from protecting the public interest." - Senator Edmund S. Muskie

Championing a tax appeal brings about an equalization of value. The property tax appeal is the means to ensure that fairness, not overpayment, and just contribution, not arbitrary assessment, result from the funding of budgetary obligations.

Yearly Revaluation Districts

Some state's statutes require a mass revaluation yearly, every two years or every 6 years. Most changes in assessments in these districts reflect inflation or deflation in the housing market. The assessor's office, because of budgetary restraints and lack of manpower, may only inspect a small portion of properties yet must place a value on each property annually.

"Studies" of property sales are used for assigning values to all properties. In states that do not employ a mass appraisal process, they must depend upon their local assessors to value all the properties. This frequent attempt at valuation places an impossible burden on the tax assessor and becomes an unattainable goal to reach. To expedite matters, the property is viewed only by the "windshield appraisal approach" and previous values are merely re-recorded thereby compounding errors. Unrealistic assessments occur.

Often the property is <u>not even seen</u> and previous years' values are simply rolled over in order to finish the task. When your property is reassessed or its classification changed, the assessor will, in most cases, mail a "Notice of Valuation" informing you of the new valuation.

129

Property Record Cards

Your property record card can be found at the municipal tax assessor's office, and you should obtain a photo copy. In some tax districts, the tax assessor will not let you see the property record card until 1 week, 10 days (or a restricted period of time) before your appeal date. They may not let you photocopy information, so be prepared to hand copy the information you will need.

While you are there, try to get the tax assessor's total square foot figures from the property record cards for the comparables you'll be using. Don't be surprised if you are turned down. If so, you will, most likely, have to resort to collecting information from a real estate agency using data derived from sold listings.

M.L.S. (Multiple Listing Service) is a system by which real estate brokers share information with each other in order to gain a greater exposure for their clients. Square foot data and other pertinent information is recorded for every property listed and sold. It would make for a stronger case, though, if you had the tax assessor's square foot computations for your comparables because then you will be working with a common set of figures.

Property record card calculations are often inaccurate because of human error in data collection and because of copying mistakes. Make certain that lot and home dimensions are correct. Often the square footage of a garage or porch is erroneously included in the total living space square footage.

Living space is taxed at a substantially higher rate than unheated, non-living space. Even a simple 2-foot error in recording the dimensions of a house could result in a 10%

overcharge. For example, a two-story raised ranch was inaccurately measured 22' x 45' when it should have measured 20' x 45'. Uneven terrain or obstacles like oil tanks or bushes increase the likelihood of sloppy measurements. Often it is much simpler for the tax collector to carry forward measurements from other previously collected data.

Check for errors in building description; it may not correctly describe your house. Tax appraisers' worksheets may have missed defects that would reduce the value of your house such as settling which results in the foundation cracking or shifting. Unfinished attics or basements may be mistakenly recorded in the room count description.

Other errors may include failure to discount negative on-site conditions or off-site influences, inaccurate description of the workmanship and quality of improvement, easement restrictions (a right or privilege that someone else may have to the land, usually limited to a specific purpose) may not be accounted for, extent of deterioration or structural defects may not be reflected in the condition of the building, quality of construction is rated as very good but may only be good or average.

If you happen to have wild kids who have wrecked the house or if termites and carpenter ants have infiltrated the house, perhaps the "average" condition rating the tax assessor gave your home should be changed. You may want to scrutinize your property record card carefully for errors. Check every entry, all measurements and descriptions, and recalculate all the math. Any disparities found can be brought before the tax assessor for review.

Possible Areas of Factual Error on Property Record Cards

measurement of house	basement
measurement of lot	basement entry
multiplication errors	crawl-space
addition errors	finished basement
number of bedrooms	unfinished basement
number of bathrooms	attic finish
special features	siding, brick or stone
type of construction	hardwood floors, slab
class of construction	heating/cooling
garage size	number of plumbing fixtures
built-in appliances	fireplace(s)
carport/canopy	porches/deck/patio
swimming pools	sheds
hot tub/sauna/greenhouse	paving
foundation material	exterior and interior wall finish
interior wall finish	sq. ft. calculations, 1st and 2nd floor
non-living space calculations	cost per square foot calculations
total land value	total building value calculation
amount of depreciation	number of stories
condition of neighborhood	quality of landscaping
construction quality rating	demolition of structure(s) not noted
External adverse effects:	*Internal adverse factors:*
unfavorable zoning	inadequate insulation
poor air quality	poor floor design
inadequate service	aluminum wiring
high housing surplus	lack of storage space
high crime rate	structural defects
poorly rated schools	antiquated plumbing and heating
infestation of insect or rodent life	noise pollution

Market value, however, is the real test for value, not property record cards (*which use a cost approach*). Research on a large sample of appraisals by appraisers in 33 states showed that an estimate derived through a cost approach was higher than the actual sale price by 9.76%.[82] This measure based on direct evidence shows the unreliability of using the cost approach alone. Further statistical tests showed that "no significant correlation exists between the cost approach appraisal variance and the age of the subject property. These results indicate that the cost approach does not result in more accurate value estimates for residential appraisals."[83]

Cost approach variance by age of property

Age	Number of Houses Samples	Average Variance
1-3 years	46	+8.9%
4-6 years	73	+10.9%
7-9 years	59	+12.6%
10-12 years	48	+9.3%
13-15 years	23	+5.3%
Over 15 years	71	+8.5%

You may catch errors in the recording of data which would result in a lowering of your assessment. Nonetheless, in order to determine the true worth of your residence and property at the annual assessment date, use the market value approach.

TAX EXEMPTIONS

The issue of taxability deals with certain types of tax exemptions. The exemption is subtracted from the assessed value before the taxes are calculated. If it is a percentage, multiply your assessed value by the percentage and subtract the result from the total assessed value. The amounts and rules vary from county to county, state to state, so check the personal exemption(s) to which you are entitled. For example, in 1991, 26% of the market value of real estate property in New York was exempt from taxation and of the remaining parcels, one in every five parcels received some type of exemption.(94) The following are fairly common types of exemptions:

Basic Homestead Exemption: Exists in most states and is usually a standard deduction from the value of the home before the tax rate is applied (e.g. the first $25,000 of assessed value).

Household Items: In states that tax personal property, certain basic household items may be exempt (e.g. range, refrigerator, furniture, etc.).

Farm or Agricultural Exemption: May require a minimum amount of earnings per year to qualify (e.g. $500) and serves to reduce the tax on property used for agricultural purposes.

Elderly Exemption: Special consideration granted to homeowners upon reaching a certain age (ages vary).

Widow's Exemption: May apply to widows or to a select group (e.g. widows of policemen, firemen, veterans).

Exemption for the Blind or Disabled: Additional homestead and school exemption for taxpayers with certain type disabilities. There may be taxable gross income limitations.

"Circuit Breaker" Relief: Tailored to benefit low-income homeowners, triggered when property tax bill exceeds a percentage of homeowner's income.

Disabled Veteran's Exemption: Offered to the disabled veteran homeowner.

Veteran's Exemption: Reduced dollar amount of taxes to military service veteran homeowners.

Surviving Spouse of a Veteran: Exemption for surviving spouse whose husband/wife served in the military and received an honorable discharge.

Surviving Spouse with Minor Children: A widow or widower property owner with a minor child or children.

School Tax Exemption: Relieves homeowner of the obligation to pay property taxes in the local school district.

Unincorporated areas: Properties located in unincorporated areas are usually exempt from paying taxes for services they don't use. These varying services may include garbage collection, water and sewage connections, street maintenance, fire and police protection, etc.

Historic Residence: Assessment freeze for historic buildings used as residences.

Improvements: Solar, hydroelectric (utilizes kinetic power of moving water), geothermal (utilizes natural heat from the earth), wind energy systems, insulation and other energy conservation measures, fallout shelters, improvements for household members who are disabled, etc.

Religious Exemption: Generally applies to the church but may apply to minister's or spouse's residence or the property of a minister or spouse who is retired or impaired.

Rehabilitated or Redeveloped Property: Applies to property that has been rehabilitated, remodeled or repaired or the property located on real property that has been redeveloped. In rehabilitated areas, this includes real estate upon which a prior existing structure was demolished to allow for new construction.

Business Investment Exemption: Provides for a partial exemption from property taxes for commercial and industrial facilities that have been altered, improved or built since a certain date and/or is in excess of a certain amount (that amount may be quite low e.g. $10,000 in NY and worth looking into if zoning is in your favor).

Mobile Home Exemption: May be eligible for reduced dollar amount of taxes.

Again, check with your municipal tax assessor or the county tax office to obtain the exemptions available in your state and municipality which apply to your particular situation.

CHAPTER 7: THE HUMAN FACTOR: NAVIGATING THE ASSESSMENT SYSTEM

"When you are betting on the outcome of a beauty contest, don't bet on the girl you think is prettiest, bet on the girl others think is prettiest." - John Maynard Keynes

PROCEEDING WITH THE PAPERWORK

A paper presentation of your appeal should have the following information for maximum effect:

1. Cover page with address, block and lot number, assessments, residential market value multiplied by sales ratio = new assessed value conclusion. High-light conclusion with a magic marker.

2. Residential market analysis.

3. Addendum, if applicable. Comments on subject's condition, comments on market data or conditions, repair cost estimates, etc.

4. Exterior dimensions of your residence showing calculation of total square feet of living space.

5. Photocopy of a Hagstrom map identifying location of subject and three comparative sale properties.

6. Pictures of subject including front angle view (showing one side of the house), rear angle view (showing the other side of the house), a street view (showing a view of the street and neighboring houses) and pictures of three comparable sales showing only a frontal view.

More information in the form of attachments can also be provided such as:

- Neighborhood boundary map
- Plat or plot plan
- FEMA Flood Insurance Rate Map
- Interior sketch with room dimensions
- Additional exterior photographs
- Interior photographs
- Legal description of subject and comparables
- Addendum of comments to justify value of adjustments
- Survey
- Photographs of off-site influences
- Contractor estimates
- Traffic survey, noise statistics, environmental study, etc.
- Evidence from private or governmental studies

Diagram example: total living space

For greater visible access to these images, copy and paste into browser:
http://www.propertytaxax.com/amazon/total-livingspace.htm

First Floor

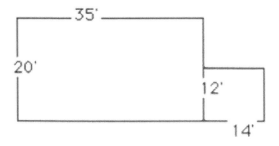

Computation of total square feet:

20' x 35' = 700 sq. ft.
12' x 14' = 168 sq. ft.

Second Floor

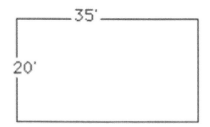

20' x 35' = 700 sq. ft.
total square feet = 1,568 sq. ft.

What <u>Not To</u> Direct Any Focus On

- comparison to past assessments
- percentage of increase
- the amount of the taxes
- the tax rate
- properties in other taxing jurisdictions
- services rendered or not rendered

• additional metropolitan costs
• inability to pay taxes

These issues cited above are not relevant to your assessment. Your assessment **must to be based on the fair market value of your property**, the most probable price that a property will sell for in a free market of buyers and sellers, free from constraining pressures or unusual situations.

"Your chances of merging into a line of traffic increase if you make eye contact with a driver in the line." - Bob Horton

THE INFORMAL MEETING WITH THE TAX ASSESSOR

Assessments are presumed to be correct. In most states (California may be the only exception), the burden of proof is on the taxpayer to challenge the assessment. The procedure for filing an appeal varies, but generally it may be a good idea to bring your appraisal findings to the attention of your local tax assessor. Find out if you have to file a formal appeal before setting up an informal hearing. Many jurisdictions have provisions for informal hearings if a formal appeal is not filed. In some states this may involve a County Tax Review Board sometimes composed of the same members as your town council. Pay special attention to the filing deadline!

Call your local tax assessor to set up a time to discuss your assessment. By this time you may have spoken to the tax assessor for his opinion of value for some of the adjustments you have been contemplating. Most tax assessors are competent people just trying to do their job. They realize that inequities exist because they do not have the staff to conduct comprehensive individual assessments. Some tax assessors, however, can be difficult and will never agree with you because they think their job is to preserve the aggregate tax base.

When presenting your case to the tax assessor, remember that they are concerned with the assessment, not the taxes. Remember you are dealing with a human being, and the impression you make is important. If your records are well organized and complete, the tax assessor will be more apt to conclude that your claim has substance.

Careless or sloppy records may be cause for the tax assessor to bias his efforts in searching for errors and in scrutinizing your value determinations. Be calm, cordial, and present the evidence in a business-like, non-threatening manner. Such a professional demeanor may give you the benefit of the doubt on issues where you have incomplete documentation.

Organize your material and keep a mental list of the items you wish to discuss. Be courteous and maintain a conversational atmosphere while presenting your evidence. You might begin with an overview of your presentation by stating, "I have conducted a residential market analysis of my property and I'd like to review my findings with you."

Before you present him with the comparables you have selected, discuss with the tax assessor the discrepancies or errors, if any, that you have found on the property record card. Be sure you have fully scrutinized what probably is the only record the tax assessor has of your property. The best chances for a reduction settlement in this informal appeal would probably be because of a mechanical or factual error on the property record card, i.e.. wrong square footage, etc.

Show him the comparables you have selected. Present him with photos of the comparables to convince him of how similar they are to your home in design, location, quality of construction, age, etc. Ask him, "These properties are viable comparables and are the closest "sold" houses similar to mine in terms of style, number of bedrooms, age, etc. Are they good comparables in your opinion also?" If he agrees, present him with your market analysis.

If he does not agree, try to convince him that the comparables you have chosen are the most recent sales in your area, that they are closest to the annual assessment date and are equivalent to your home in most categories. Ask him, for instance, if they are similar in style, location, number of rooms, etc. It is important to have your assessor agree that the comparables you have selected are similar to your home. Once you have firmly established in the tax assessor's mind that equivalent comparable sales were chosen, he will have to base his decision solely on the market value arrived at using those comparables upon which you have done your homework.

The assessor is compelled to challenge all appeals by the taxpayer and it may be difficult to change the assessor's mind when presenting your evidence. An antagonistic attitude on your part may push the tax assessor to challenge your adjustment claims more severely. Beware of irrelevant trick questions that the assessor may pose and tell him that the question does not coincide with the information you found. Your answers to seemingly innocent questions may tip off the tax assessor to new areas to investigate in which you may not be prepared to answer. Don't volunteer more information than is necessary.

If you are addressing an adjustment, such as an environmental issue, emphasize the perceived loss in value as seen through the eyes of a typical buyer. Show the market reaction by finding comparables suffering the same distress locationally as yours. Buyers, in all likelihood, will find hidden defects either through disclosure statements, home inspections or through direct experience. Misrepresentation by the seller could result in legal action. Why not make an adjustment for your house's loss in value especially since you will be penalized for defects if you sell it?

As you proceed with the residential market analysis form, discuss each adjustment that affects the value of your house. Keep in mind that the value of your adjustments are subjective and the assessor might not agree with you on the dollar value of each and every item. Write in the amount he agrees to. Leave a copy with him for his reference.

When you present the information you have gathered, include photographs of your residence and comparables. Pictures speak a thousand words and care should be taken to obtain the whole house within the frame of the picture, not the size of the yard dwarfing the house. It is only necessary to photograph the front of the comparables, but include a front and rear picture of the subject (your residence) to reaffirm your assertions. Also include a diagram of your residence reflecting the total square feet. Use only measurements taken from the outside of your house in your calculations.

The tax assessor routinely refers to the property record card and data you've presented. Most decisions are not given immediately. Ask him what the next step is. You may have to file a formal appeal even if the assessor agrees with you. Also, the assessor may have to request permission from the County Tax Board to enter a revision. The tax assessor will usually say that he'll get back to you in a few days with an opinion. After you meet to receive

143

his opinion, you can still try to wrangle for a lower assessment. If you do reach an agreement, get it in writing. The process of recording the agreement could be interrupted and forgotten or facts improperly remembered.

The tax assessor would prefer to make a settlement at his level than to have to involve the County Tax Review Board. Also, there is time-consuming extra work in preparing your rebuttal to consider. If you receive a settlement, you will be notified by mail of your new assessment and any tax refund plus interest due to you. If you have a mortgage, your mortgage company will be notified and you will be credited with the tax savings.

Also, you can always request a new individual reassessment, and if you feel the new reassessment is biased, you have the right to appeal that, too. Entire neighborhood reassessments can be initiated by the residents. If you are to be reassessed, you will receive notice indicating the time of the inspection. It is important that you be there with the inspector to point out areas of depreciation, deterioration, or any areas that you feel affect the marketability of your property. If you do not let the assessor into your house, he will assign a value to your home equivalent to the highest similar valued house he can find.

Finally, while you are at the assessor's office, find out if you qualify for any exemptions.

THE COUNTY TAX REVIEW BOARD

"The average bull lasts 20 minutes in a bullfight." - L.M. Boyd, *The San Francisco Chronicle*

If no results come out of your encounter with the tax assessor, you should appeal to the County Tax Board (may be called the Board of Review, County Board of Taxation, Board of Equalization, etc.). Be sure to respond by the proper filing date. The appeal process begins when the assessment notices are sent out, and it is your responsibility to respond by deadline dates. Obtain a copy of the particular instructions for filing an appeal petition and copies of the filing forms from the County Board of Taxation or ask your tax assessor where you can obtain them.

Be sure to file your original petition with the County Tax Board and any copies that may be required by the municipal tax assessor and clerk of your municipality as specified in your instruction form. **Be sure to read the preparation instructions carefully**. Heed time restraints.

In some states you may have to include copies of your residential market analysis and copies of photographs of your property and the comparables (sometimes 3 or more copies, one for each board member) at least 1 week before the hearing or within the time restraints given by the County Tax Board. These extra copies for review board members are so they can follow your line of evidence when you have the opportunity to present it. Make sure your taxes are paid up to date; failure to comply may result in dismissal of your petition.

After filing your petition, you will receive notice through the mail of your hearing date. Adjournments (postponements) are not granted unless under extraordinary circumstances. Try to attend an appeal board hearing before your scheduled date to get a feel for what to expect.

When you arrive at the location of the public hearing, your attendance will be noted. The town will usually hire an attorney to represent the town. The town tax assessor and town attorney will be present at the hearing in an adversarial role to challenge your evidence wherever they can. When you are called to testify, you will be sworn in. Your judges will be the members of the Tax Review Board (be they one or 20 in number).

The board usually consists of 3-5 members who have a knowledge of property values. Members are appointed by the legislative body (town board, city council, etc.) of the local government. The tax assessor and town attorney are not part of the Board of Review since the Board of Review's purpose is to ensure that you receive an impartial decision. Using a boxing match as an example, it is you against the tax assessor and town attorney with the Review Board judging, deciding the match. Theoretically, it is **the facts that rule**, not the board and not the assessor.

You will undoubtedly have the opportunity to listen to other people appealing their assessments before you and to become somewhat more familiar for what the Board of Review is looking. The average meeting lasts only 10 to 15 minutes. When you have your turn, read your prepared 'appraisal' presenting only the information that supports your case to the members of the appraisal board.

Remember: the appeal board members are the ones who decide the case on the county level, not the adversarial tax assessor or the town attorney. Never tell the board or the tax assessor that you are appealing your taxes - you are appealing your assessment. You are seeking equalization in assessment to similar properties such as yours.

How to make a more memorable presentation

- **Plant your feet.** Adjust the mike if necessary. Scan the members of the review board audience. Speak to the person furthest away so your voice reaches them.

- **Begin with a very short story or an observation.** Use the words "a few hours ago," "a week ago," "a month ago" "a year ago" etc. "it occurred to me that my property taxes were out of whack and I needed to do something ... " as a hook and tell a short story if time permits.

- **Radiate authority.** Pause after each sentence. Put rhythm in the tempo of your sentences as you emphasize each set of facts.

- **Finish with an overview.** "The evidence I have presented can be distilled into a final value conclusion of ..." Leave them with a definite impression of the final value. Don't let your voice trail off.

See www.toastmasters.org or www.clearcommunicaton.com for more public speaking tips.

"I'm proud to be paying taxes in the United States. The only thing is, I could be just as proud for half the money." - Arthur Godfrey

Your adversaries (the tax assessor and town attorney) may try to question your expert witness status. You can reply that there is no one better qualified than yourself to be an expert witness in your own neighborhood.

You've lived there for years, have traveled the streets and compared other neighborhoods to your own, scrutinized improvements and detractions, attended "open houses" hosted by real estate agents, witnessed comparable properties that were bought and sold. You've analyzed and reviewed all the comparable houses that sold in the last year listed in the Multiple Listing Service "sold" directory. You've absorbed and complied to rules, regulations and guidelines set by the Federal National

147

Mortgage Association (FNMA or Fanny Mae), the Federal Housing Authority as well as other Federal agencies (Farmers Home Administration or FmHA), etc. by using acceptable market valuation rules and principles.

You've consulted real estate agents, appraisers and/or the tax assessor in your local area for determinations on questionable items of value. You know what contractors charge for a specific enhancement, you know how to calculate depreciation. You have supporting evidence for all your adjustments. So, in what area do you lack expertise?

The attorney for the town or the town tax assessor may try to point out contradictions, oversights or poor estimations of value based on the information they have uncovered. They may use questions of little importance or insinuations in an attempt to get a hurried reply that can be used against you. For instance: they may try to imply that the purchase price or the amount for what the house is insured is a valid representation of market price. This type of reasoning is irrelevant to the fair market price.

Only a market analysis earmarking a specific time period, using similar and comparable properties, is a supportable and valid method for determining probable selling price. By using the market value approach, you can be an expert in your own neighborhood in determining the market value of your home. Remember, who is better qualified than you since you live and observe the neighborhood influences daily? The only contentious issue should be the value of an individual adjustment.

They may want to show that you have chosen poor comparables, are unfamiliar with the comparables, not sure of the adjustments, that you are foolish or incompetent. Have an idea about what you are going to say before you speak, and let there be no doubt in your audience's mind (or your own!) that you are certain of the facts. Expect interruptions from the opposing town attorney when they do not like the testimony you are giving. If the town attorney gets argumentative and makes you feel uncomfortable, you can object to the Tax Board that you are indeed being harassed or at least that the town attorney is being argumentative.

"Fate loves the fearless."(83) The success of your appeal depends on the impression of believability just as much as it depends on the facts and supporting evidence. You have to confidently assert the facts without lecturing, showing disrespect or becoming emotional. Eye contact with the Board of Review is mandatory. In public speaking, the best way to reduce your nervousness is to be thorough in your preparation and well rehearsed. Be completely familiar with the facts.

The tax assessor is unusually burdened this time of the year and may not have chosen representative comparables or spent much time preparing evidence. Often his adjustments are poorly derived or are inappropriate or incomplete. Point out and question any un-similar characteristics. Point out differences in date of sale, location, site, or any feature that is not comparable to yours.

Challenge the assessor for a written copy of the comparables he has chosen. Ask the tax assessor how he arrived at an adjustment. Ask for figures, rattle his cage for specifics. If his square footage figures appear questionable, ask if they include the dimensions of the garage, porch, attic (if they have these features). Ask to see photographs of the comparable properties he has chosen. **In most every case, the tax assessor doesn't have any**; it is not their practice to take pictures. Refer to your photos, evidence ... as being the best.

149

You must be able to show that the value judgment the tax assessor placed on your property was in error. If the town attorney cannot discredit your major points, he may try to exaggerate minor points. Listen carefully, speak carefully. Explain if there are inaccuracies, computational errors, or mistakes in the property record card, and proceed with the residential market analysis underscoring each value adjustment. For example, emphasize that the comparables you have chosen are the most recent in date of sale to the assessment date and most similar to your residence because they mirror a similar neighborhood, exemplify a similar number of bedrooms, typify similar square footage, etc. Be sure you can back up your facts to be credible.

Be confident in presenting your case, speak with clarity and with conviction, look at those you address in the eye. You'll sound and appear more believable. If you can cast doubt on the other side's opinion, your evidence will gain value swaying the tide to your point of view. Do not exaggerate or make inaccurate statements. Finish by leaving the board with an impression, a dollar figure, of what the assessment should be. Clearly emphasize the final dollar value. Your conversation may be recorded for later review by board members.

"Thought is better than words, because it guides them." - Sholem Aleichem

What to Focus On in a Property Tax Appeal

- Areas that the board will address.
- Be familiar with the facts
- Practice your appeal so it is clear and well thought out.
- Engage in a courteous, conversational manner.

- Bring evidence, i.e. contractor's estimates if you claim your house is in poor condition; traffic study and pictures of bus's, congestion, etc. if you are going to claim a relatively high level of traffic; evidence from private or governmental studies, scientific criteria, etc.
- Emphasize areas of similarity to your residence from your comparables.
- Point out any differences in the tax assessor's comparables for location, site influence, etc.
- Ask assessor how adjustments for questionable comparables were arrived at.
- Ask to see tax assessor's picture for a comparable (most likely he has no pictures).
- Ask for a copy of the comparables that the tax assessor has chosen (most likely he has no copy).
- Ask if the assessor's square footage totals include the garage, porch, attached shed etc. (unheated areas).
- If there exists an environmental adjustment, emphasize, "would you pay the same price for a house next to a known high EMF power transmission line, unsightly water tower, road noise etc, if you could buy a house not plagued with that problem? Any knowledgeable buyer will discount negative areas and offer less money because of the property's liabilities."
- Emphasize dollar value on items you address.
- Stick to the facts.

Optional Props

Charts: You may find it easier to use a large white chart listing only those items for which adjustments are recorded. List superior features and inferior features for each comparable. Each member of the board already has a copy of the residential market analysis and this prop will focus on the crux of the appeal. If the tax assessor uses other comparables, ask to see a written copy of the comparables he is using.

Often an incomplete analysis is presented by the opposition producing a sketchy, shoddy valuation that is full of holes. Find the holes and expose them. It is you who are the authority of your property and neighborhood. You live there, drive through it constantly and are more likely to note changes than anyone else. Focus attention back on the adjustments of your chart and be prepared to back up your figures. You'll appear better prepared with a highlighted chart, and if you have the facts and avoid the opposition's undermining of your adjustment conclusion, you will win.

Pictures: By having enlargements of pictures for demonstration and mounting them on a ridged surface, you may gain an advantage. You can often refer to them in your presentation. Using pictures, illustrate your point to the Board of Adjustments or use the pictures to point out to the opposing tax assessor any details or information that make your point stronger.

Calculators: If you are somewhat skilled at using a calculator, you can nail down the opposition's errors. The board members may not be strong mathematically, and by revealing your skill, your credibility is enhanced.

Hearing Deliberations

Don't take the first carrot! Often the tax assessor will make an offer for settlement before the hearing proceeds. This is usually because of weakness in his or her case. Don't be too quick to take this offer. In most instances, you will receive a more favorable settlement by presenting your case to the Review Board.

Give it your best shot; don't let yourself be unnerved. The tax assessor and review board members are paid to look at your facts, and the facts rule! If you have done an accurate job and have the evidence to support your adjustments, you can take your appeal to the top and win. Although your part is over at the completion of the hearing, the Board will not make its decision immediately, and most likely you will be notified of the Board's action in a few weeks.

If, after appealing your case, you discover that you made a mistake or overlooked something that made a significant difference, you can re-appeal next year. Evidence submitted at the hearing is part of the public record and, at a minimum charge, is available for your review. The appeal process does not change, and it will be much easier and more coherent the second time. Appeal fees are minimal, and you can keep on appealing your assessment until you are successful.

In the interim, by completing a residential market analysis, you will have uncovered the true market value for your homestead and also have discovered the true assessed value for your house. You will have the liberty of time to observe and select recent sales in your community to use as comparables in your new appeal. Before real estate sales are finalized, you will have the opportunity to walk through, measure and familiarize yourself with comparable homes in your neighborhood.

When you win your case, the County Board of Taxation is required to send you a notification (memorandum of judgment). This notice of valuation will show you the original assessment alongside a judgment for your new, lower assessment.

"The man who persists in knocking will succeed in entering." - Moses Ibn Ezra

153

JUDICIAL REVIEW, STATE BOARD OF EQUALIZATION, STATE TAX COURT

If you are not satisfied with the decision of the Review Board, you can carry your appeal one step higher to the State Appeal Board or Judicial Review (also may be called the State Board of Equalization or State Tax Court). This is usually the final step in the appeal process and there are similar specific steps to follow to preserve your appeal rights when appealing to the courts. Go to the State Appeal Board if you feel you have a strong case. The tax assessor (the same one with whom you have been dealing) will try to negotiate with you at this point rather than incur the serious costs associated with dragging in the town attorney and generating public exposure. At this level of review, they will know that you are very serious.

Again, attend one hearing to observe the proceedings so you may learn what to expect. Understand the order of presentation and the rules particular to your state that you are expected to follow. There is usually a pamphlet available as a guide. Your presentation will be similar to the presentation to the Review Board except that, in this case, you are seeking to overturn the decision of the Review Board and the local tax assessor.

The official(s) who will hear your case is (are) most likely unfamiliar with your neighborhood. They will be concerned strictly with the facts used to establish market value. You can gather more facts to support your case but you cannot create a new case. Usually, you cannot change your appeal for a lower assessment and must stick to your original claim. As evidence for your appeal, you may need to hire a fee appraiser to further validate your findings. Check with your state rules to see if your prepared residential market analysis is sufficient. If not, is there a requirement for an appraiser to testify in person or does the appraiser need to meet state license requirements?

Want to increase your chances of a refund by 37% (or more)? Well, here's a hot tip found in a study conducted by the Lincoln Institute of Land Policy; Rochester, NY (reported in 2001 by Investors Business Daily)

- Only 2% of homeowners in the NY area, according to a study conducted by the Lincoln Institute of Land Policy, carried their appeal beyond the local assessor.
- Those that took the case to the local assessor won an average reduction of 8%.
- Those that went further to the municipal tax court achieved an average reduction of 13% off their home tax assessment.
- Those that went the distance to the New York Supreme Court had 37% of their home tax assessment rolled back.

TAX APPEAL ALTERNATIVES

If you do not want to research the facts and present your case personally, the alternative 'Cadillac' approach would be to hire a lawyer to represent you before the board and an appraiser to deliver testimony in the capacity of an expert witness. Even if you hire an appraiser to represent you, you may be required personally to be present according to many tax boards. Appraisers' fees range between $200-$500 for an assignment and usually require an extra $200-$500 to appear before the board and testify on your behalf.

Attorneys can charge at least 10 times the average working person's hourly wages (billing for secretarial services at the same rate) for their service. They'll speak at the hearing for 5 to 10 minutes and will most likely charge for an entire day.

In some states and counties, it may be permissible to have a tax consultant represent you. His\her fees are usually on a contingency basis, and it costs you nothing if he is not successful in your appeal. Fees are typically 50% of the first year's tax savings and then a smaller percentage, usually 25% of your tax savings for the next 2 years.

"If cats wore gloves, they wouldn't catch mice." - Anon.

DISCREET STATE AND MUNICIPAL PRACTICES

In order to inconvenience those appealing their property taxes, legislation in some states creates stumbling blocks. For instance, corporations, for the most part, may be required to be represented by attorneys, increasing the expense to the appellant. The attorney, in most instances, has no expertise in valuation and may have little or no exposure to the real estate market. Any small entrepreneur's profit or non-profit corporation is penalized by this restrictive practice. "100 million Americans cannot afford basic legal help. Yet the ABA (American Bar Association) and its affiliate state bar associations are unwilling to seriously entertain any solution that doesn't let the legal profession continue to limit competition."(82)

Private citizens desiring to appeal their taxes are sometimes stymied by laws that eliminate their choice to have cost-effective professionals represent their interest. Tax consultants, who charge only if the appeal is successful, may be prevented from obtaining clients because the power of attorney is limited to those licensed to practice law in that particular state. In non-restrictive states, a tax consultant can be helpful. However, a property tax consultant will unwittingly pursue the path of justice by an appeal only if he or she feels there is a significant reduction to be gained in favor of the taxpayer.

In judicially restrictive states, an attorney would be necessary for representation if you do not desire to speak up for yourself. Attorneys do not determine the market value of your home, therefore, a real estate appraiser would be consulted, further exacerbating the cost of the appeal.

Rather than relying on a professionally prepared report that properly analyzes the property in question, the town relies on a problematic mass appraisal or the tax assessor's lickety-split reckoning. Yet, when it comes to required evidence, the town may require the presence of state licensed appraisers at the tax hearing instead of relying on a written appraisal alone. Appraisers may feel they are worth $500+ a day and charge extra to hang around for what may amount to an entire day in order to read a 5 to 10 minute report.

For the individual property owner, **the only economical recourse in most circumstances is to champion his or her own appeal**. The purpose of this book is to make this process clear, instructive and manageable in order to increase equitability among victims of unjust valuation.

CHAPTER 8 : IN CONCLUSION: A PROFESSIONAL PRESENTATION

"The whole is equivalent to the sum of its parts." - additive law

The following restates what information a proper tax appeal should contain and how it is arranged in order of presentation:

1. Cover page with address, block and lot number, assessments, residential market value multiplied by sales ratio = new assessed value conclusion. Highlight final value with transparent color ink.

2. Residential market analysis page.

3. Addendum to residential market analysis. Comments on subject's condition, comments on market data, locational deficiencies, repair cost estimates, etc.

4. Diagram of exterior dimensions of your residence showing total square feet. A scale drawing is not necessary. This gives a good visual reinforcement of your home and its living and non-living space.

5. Photocopy of a Hagstrom map identifying location of subject and the three comparative sale properties.

6. Pictures of the subject including front angle view (showing the side of the house), rear angle view (showing the other side of the house) and a street view.

7. Pictures of three comparable sales showing only a front view. Subject photos should be displayed first followed by those of the comparable sales.

EXAMPLE OF COVER PAGE VALUE CONCLUSION

Joe and Mary Smith
5 Walrus Lane
Mongoose, CA 12345
Crocodile Twp., Critter County, CA
Block 21 Lot

Current Assessed Land Value $25,100

Current Assessed Improved Value $193,000

Current Assessed Total Value $218,100

Appraised Value as of 10/1/06 $301,000

Sales Ratio 51.7

Suggested Assessed Value **$155,600**

EXAMPLE OF A RESIDENTIAL MARKET ANALYSIS

Since this is a larger graph than will fit in this location, view this analysis sheet at:
http://propertytaxax.com/amazon/rma.htm

ADDENDUM TO RESIDENTIAL MARKET ANALYSIS

Here is where one presents pertinent information, if applicable, on subject's condition, comments on locational deficiencies, contractor's estimates, cost estimate figures, traffic survey, opinions from relevant authorities, etc.) This can be pages long. An example follows:

Highlight the category that you are going to elaborate on. Detail your support evidence. For example:

Site Adjustment: (Location and view adjustment reconciled at this location)

Although the site has more square footage than the comparables, most of the property **is inaccessible because of a steep downhill mountain slope** at the rear of the lot. Only a small front portion of the lot is available for use.

1) Subject property is located **170 feet from Route 23**, a heavily traveled major 4 lane highway connecting to Route 80. Subject is victim to extremely loud road noise during morning and evening rush hour. Weekend traffic noise is also loud and annoying. The Sunday noise level for the rush to get back to the cities reaches highly irritable proportions most of the day. It builds to a crescendo in the afternoon and evening hours. The population density is not sufficient to petition the state for the erection of noise barriers.

2) Also the subject property is **32 feet from 230 kilovolt high-tension electrical towers**. (The lot is 32 feet from the right of way to PSE&G towers. An 18.4 mG reading (2 or more mG reading is considered high) under these lines was obtained by an JCP&L engineer.

Ugly high tension towers and high tension lines are an eye sore and obstruct a normal view. They also invite skepticism and place a stigma on the property value. The not-in-my-back-yard (NIMBY) syndrome affects purchasing decisions and, therefore, lowers my property value.

Because of the excessive road noise and ugly electrical towers for the subject property, a negative $42,000 adjustment has been made to the comparable properties.

Comparable 1 & 2 enjoy a quiet street and normal residential view. Comparable 3 is located on a nice corner lot 1 block from Packanack with a winter view of the lake.

Functional Utility Subject property has an abnormal low ceiling height in the bedroom, throughout the house as well as in the entrance area. Ceiling height reaches 6 foot 2 inches in the bedroom, 6 foot 4 inches at the entrance foyer and 6 foot 2 inches in the living room area. An average 8-foot ceiling height is the role for most houses. This is a major structural negative and accounts for a substantial proportion of the house.

A negative $7,500 adjustment has been made to compensate for this deficiency that the subject property does not enjoy.

Quality of Construction Comparable 2 has been remodeled with new roof, interior, siding, remodeled interior, new kitchen cabinets, appliances, carpet.

Subject property has a deteriorating roof, rotting wood around exterior window moldings, pealing paint and dented aluminum siding. Interior carpets need replacing, cabinets are dated, needs painting.

A negative $19,000 adjustment has been made to compensate for this deficiency that the subject property does not enjoy.

Gross Living Area
Comparables have varying gross living areas. A conservative $80 sq./ft replacement cost adjustment was used for Comp 1 and 2. Comp 3 is of a log construction

161

and $55 sq./ft multiplier for comp. 3 to reflect the less expensive, log construction.

A positive $13,040 adjustment has been made to Comp. 1 in order to compensate for this.

A positive $2,160 adjustment has been made to Comp. 2 in order to compensate for this.

A negative $8,720 adjustment has been made to Comp. 3 in order to compensate for this that the subject property does not enjoy.

Heating and Cooling Comparable 3 has electric heat while the subject has HWBB.

A positive $5,500 adjustment has been made to compensate for this feature that the subject property enjoys in relation to the comparable's deficiency.

Improper Tax Assessor Square Foot Calculation Tax assessor square foot calculations for the subject property included a 20-ft x 20-ft non-heated attached shed.

Heated square footage for subject property should read: **1,547.24 square feet**

EXAMPLE OF EXTERIOR DIMENSION SKETCH ADDENDUM

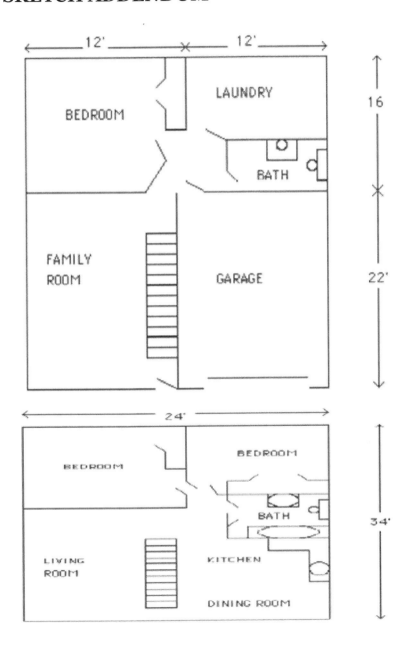

First Floor Plan = 912 square feet. Second Floor Plan =
816 sq. ft. Total Square Feet = 1,728 sq. ft.

HAGSTROM MAP IDENTIFICATIONS

Make a photocopy of a map and indicate the location of
the subject and comparable properties. This is
accomplished by drawing or pasting pre-drawn arrows
designating locations of each property.

PHOTOGRAPH ADDENDUM FOR
SUBJECT

See representation of a photograph addendum for subject
at:
http://www.propertytaxax.com/amazon/photo-
addendum-subject.htm

PHOTOGRAPH ADDENDUM FOR
COMPARABLES

See representation of a photograph addendum for comparables
at:
http://www.propertytaxax.com/amazon/photo-addendum-
subject.htm

CHAPTER 9: AFFILIATED INFORMATION

"A large colony of Formosan subterranean termites can eat 2-3 pounds of wood a day. In a month's time, that's up to 90 pounds of wood." - researchers at University of Florida

DEPRECIATION

ESTIMATING DEPRECIATION: STRAIGHT-LINE METHOD:

While the market value comparison approach for determining the value of a particular structure is desirable, in some situations suitable comparables may not be readily available and a depreciated cost approach may be appropriate. Furthermore, in some instances, different structures on the site may vary in age. These structures may range from a deck, garage, workshop, to guest houses, tennis courts, etc.

The depreciated value calculation for that structure would be entered in the corresponding item category on the residential market analysis form. An accepted method of depreciation used by the American Institute of Real Estate Appraisers on the basis of physical life or economic life projection is the straight-line method.(87)

Three concepts need to be clarified before we focus on depreciation:

> (1) the actual age
> (2) the effective age
> (3) the economic life.

(1) The <u>actual age</u> or life of a structure is its chronological age since it has been built. The physical age is the actual age. Usually it is possible to determine when your house was built by lifting the lid on the water closet for the toilet and looking on the underside. The month, date and year of manufacture is impressed in the underside of the porcelain lid.

(2) The <u>effective age</u> is how old the structure appears to be based on condition, general upkeep and economic forces. If you have a workshop, guest house, Florida room, garage(s), etc., it is normal to assume that it has the same effective age as your house. Because the garage, for example, goes along with your house, the garage assumes the same character as the house. However, sometimes, a garage or other outside building is not re-modernized, while the house is. In that instance, it would be necessary to determine the depreciated cost of the structure that was built earlier or later.

Finding a depreciated cost of an earlier built structure would cut the value of that structure and push up the price of a later-built structure. Again, the **effective age** is the age that the building appears to be when compared to a new structure. In some situations, public tastes may change or some features may be undesirable in comparison to newer structures. If a 70-year old building was re-modernized with new wiring, new drywall, modern plumbing, etc., the effective age may deserve a 10-year age designation. In this example, we disregard the actual age and consider only the general condition to determine the effective age. Poor maintenance will create an effective age greater than the actual age of a building.

(3) The <u>economic life</u> is an estimate of how long the structure will be used. When the value of the structure contributes nothing to the value of the land, then the structure has ended its economic life.

The straight-line depreciation method assumes that deterioration takes place at a constant rate over the estimated life of an improvement or building. As a general rule, if the improvement or building is estimated to last 100 years, then it depreciates at 1% per year. For example, in 25 years it would depreciate 25%.

However, a typical effective age depreciation table is provided on the following page to show specific calculations of depreciation used by real estate appraisers. This depreciation table assumes that the economic life of this neighborhood is average by all estimates. To use this table, multiply the replacement cost (new) for the building by the total percentage of depreciation found in the effective age depreciation table. Subtract this dollar amount from the total replacement cost (new) to arrive at the current value (or the depreciated replacement cost of the structure).

For example, an average 26 year old house would incur a 35% depreciation factor. Anything attached to the home assumes the same character as the home, therefore an attached garage equally incurs the same 35% depreciation.

TYPICAL EFFECTIVE AGE DEPRECIATION TABLE (straight-line method)

EFFECTIVE AGE	POOR	LOW-FAIR	AVERAGE	GOOD	EXCELLENT	EFFECTIVE AGE
1	1%	1%	1%	0%	0%	1
2	2	2	1	1	1	2
3	2	2	2	2	2	3
4	3	3	3	2	2	4
5	5	5	4	3	3	5
6	6	6	4	4	4	6
7	7	7	5	5	5	7
8	8	8	6	6	6	8
9	10	9	7	7	6	9
10	11	11	9	8	7	10
11	13	12	10	9	8	11
12	14	13	11	10	9	12
13	16	14	12	11	10	13
14	18	16	13	12	11	14
15	20	17	15	13	12	15
16	22	19	16	14	13	16
17	24	20	17	16	14	17
18	26	22	19	17	16	18
19	28	24	20	18	17	19
20	30	25	22	20	18	20
21	32	26	24	21	19	21
22	34	28	25	22	20	22
23	36	30	26	24	21	23
24	38	32	28	25	23	24
25	40	33	30	27	24	25
26	42	35	31	28	25	26
27	44	36	33	31	27	27
28	45	38	35	31	28	28
29	47	40	36	33	29	29
30	48	41	38	34	31	30
31	50	42	40	36	32	31
32	51	44	42	38	33	32
33	53	45	44	39	35	33
34	54	47	45	41	36	34
35	55	48	46	42	37	35
36	56	49	48	43	39	36
37	57	50	49	45	40	37
38	58	52	51	46	41	38

39	59	53	52	47	42	39
40	59	54	53	49	43	40
41	60%	55%	54%	50%	45%	41
42	61	56	56	51	46	42
43	61	57	57	52	47	43
44	62	58	58	54	48	44
45	62	58	58	55	49	45
46	63	59	59	56	50	46
47	63	60	60	57	51	47
48	64	61	61	58	52	48
49	64	62	61	58	53	49
50	65	63	62	59	54	50
51		63	62	60	55	51
52		64	62	61	56	52
53		64	63	61	57	53
54		65	63	62	58	54
55		65	63	62	59	55
56			64	62	59	56
57			64	63	60	57
58			64	63	61	58
59			65	63	62	59
60			65	64	62	60
61				64	63	61
62				64	63	62
63				64	64	63
64				65	64	64
65				65	65	65

IFA Depreciation-Residential Properties Table (88) Also see:
http://www.calculatorsoup.com/calculators/financial/depreciation-straight-line.php

DEPRECIATION FOR STRUCTURES WITH SHORTER LIFE-SPANS

While the chart above gives depreciation percentages for an average house, some situations may require a shorter estimate of economic life. For instance a roof may last 20 years, a wolmanized deck 35 years, a gazebo 20 years, a macadam tennis court or driveway 18 years, a carpet 12 years, etc. The time period when a house may be profitably used ends when the land value is equal to the structure. When a structure has a short life, depreciation is accelerated.

The formula for estimating depreciation is expressed as follows:

Effective Age /Typical Economic Life = % Depreciation of Reproduction Cost

For instance, a wooden deck constructed of Douglas fir (non-pressure treated or non-wolmanized wood) is 15 years old and is weathered. Wood structures left unprotected from the weather in this region of the country last about 20 years. This particular deck has boards that are decayed due to dry-rot, popped nails and has a general condition of deteriorated wear and tear. Under these conditions, the deck merits a 18-year effective age.

170

18 years (Effective Age) / 20 years (Economic Life) = .90
or 90% depreciation

If the deck costs $3,000 to build in today's market, allowing for 90% depreciation would give us a depreciated and adjusted value of $300 for the deck.

Using another example, a structure in poor condition has an estimated effective age of 30 years because of decayed wood, a flat roof, inferior footings and a cracked slab floor. The structure has an actual, chronological age of 22 years. The economic life of the structure is estimated to be 50 years.

30 years (Effective Age) / 50 years (Economic Life) = .60
or 60% depreciation

If the replacement cost of the structure is $20,000, then it is adjusted because of a 60% depreciation thereby resulting in an $8,000 final valuation.

In another example, the replacement cost for a low-to-fair quality, framed, detached garage that was built 30 years ago is $14,000 (The replacement cost in any given region, on any given year, can be determined by information given in Marshall & Swift Residential Cost Handbook).

Assume that the roof hasn't been replaced and leaks, and the garage is in run-down condition creating an estimated effective age of 50 years. In the column for 50 effective years, a corresponding 65% depreciation factor is listed. Multiplying the replacement cost, $14,000, by the depreciation factor of 65% results in a current value of $4,900 ($14,000 - $9,100).

Projected life expectancy of American homes is very low compared to European homes. In Europe, houses last hundreds of years; however one could make an educated guess that well-built houses with good maintenance in America could last as long as those in Europe. Yet, it is almost impossible to accurately forecast the estimated life of a house and the ensuing depreciation without relying on certain underlying assumptions.

Those assumptions are that there is no change; no neglect, no new rejuvenation, no change in economic forces, no changes in design, and no new concepts or new inventions that affect the property value.

CHAPTER 10: DISCLOSURE LAWS

"Twelve cockroaches can live on the glue of a postage stamp for a week." - Austin Friedman, entomologist

DISCLOSURE LAWS FOR HOME SELLERS

Since 1984 many state courts have held that sellers must tell buyers about every substantial defect in the property of which they are aware. Real estate brokers have incurred law suits since they are usually representatives of the sellers and have promoted mandatory disclosure laws. The increase in the number of home inspection professionals is in direct response to these disclosure laws.

Mandatory disclosure laws answer questions and expose defects so that a buyer in the market knows exactly what he or she is buying. Any misrepresentation or omission can represent a costly liability to the seller. *When appealing your taxes, it would be foolish not to make adjustments to the value of your home if it suffered in any of the areas that mandatory disclosure uncovers.*

The following is the format for a typical disclosure statement.

Specimen Disclosure Statement Form (89)

State the conditions of appliances and systems including repairs within the last two years covering: range, oven, microwave, hood, fan, dishwasher, refrigerator, disposal, washer, dryer, trash compactor, central air, water softener, attic fan, sump pump, ceiling fan, TV antenna, garage door opener and remote controls, fireplace and chimney.

Property conditions and improvements:

1. Basement: Has there been evidence of problems with water leakage? If so, explain, including the frequency and extent of the problem.
2. Insulation: Describe, if known. Has urea formaldehyde foam (UFFI) insulation been installed? If removed, by whom and when?
3. Roof: Age of roof. Leaks. History of repairs.
4. Well or city water systems? If well, type of well, depth and diameter. Age of well and any known problems or repairs. Has the water been tested? Date of last test and results?
5. Septic tanks, drain fields, aeration tank, filtration bed, cesspool or city sewer system? Any known problems or repairs?
6. Heating system: type, age and any known problems or repairs?
7. Plumbing system, copper, galvanized, other. Hot water mixing valves, if any? Any known problems or repairs?
8. Electrical system: capacity, any known problems or repairs?
9. History of infestation, if any (termites, carpenter ants, etc.). Any treatment for infestation? Any unrepaired damage?
10. Asbestos: Is asbestos present in any form on the property? If yes, where? Has asbestos been removed or encapsulated? If removed, where, when (date) and by whom?
11. Radon: Has the property been tested for the presence of radon gas? What were the test results?
12. Are you aware of any other environmental concerns such as discoloration of soil or vegetation or oil sheen in wet areas? If so, describe.
13. Are you aware of any principal uses of the property

other than as residential property, such as commercial use, dumping site, farming?

Other Items:

14. Features of any property shared in common with adjoining landowners, such as walls, fences, roads and driveways whose use or responsibility for maintenance may have an effect on the property? If yes, describe.
15. Any rights-of-way, easements or similar matters that may affect your interest in the property? If yes, describe.
16. Room additions, structural modifications, or other alterations or repairs made without necessary permits or licensed contracts? If yes, please describe.
17. Settling, flooding, drainage, grading, or soil problems? If yes, describe.
18. Major damage to the property or any of the structures from fire, wind, floods or landslides? If yes, describe
19. Any zoning violations or nonconforming uses? If yes, describe.
20. Homeowners' association which has any authority over the property?
21. Any "common areas" (facilities such as pools, tennis courts, walkways, or other areas co-owned in undivided interest with others)?
22. Please state any other facts or information relating to this property that would be of concern to a buyer.

To the extent of the seller's knowledge as a property owner, the seller acknowledges that the information contained above is true and accurate for those areas of the property listed. Sign and date.

As of 2006, 30 states require home sellers to fill out mandatory standardized forms, and the majority of states have legislation pending or in review.(90)

Real Estate Disclosure Form, Property Information, Seller Disclosure Form, Sellers Disclosure Statement, Home Disclosure Form, Home Disclosure Act, Property Disclosure Law, Real Estate Disclosure Form - No matter what it's called, most states require the seller of a home to provide information to the buyer about the condition of real estate (the home). While states have different names for the form, its purpose is the same - to provide the buyer with a minimum level of information about the property being purchased. If your home and property has a disclosure defect, be sure to make an adjustment for it.

The laws typically require the seller to supply this type of information:

- Do you have legal authority to sell the property?
- Are there any encroachments, boundary agreements, or boundary disputes?
- If the property is served by a public or community sewer main, is the house connected to the main?
- Has the roof leaked? If yes, has it been repaired?
- Have there been any conversions, additions, or remodeling? If yes, were all building permits obtained?

Depending on the state, the list can be upwards of 10 pages long.

http://www.fdic.gov/consumers/consumer/rights/index.html for Federal Laws and State Laws

http://www.eli.org for specific State Disclosure Legislation

http://www.rentalagreements.com/realestate-disclosure-forms.htm for states Sellers Disclosure Statement Forms

APPENDIX B: ELECTRONIC APPRAISER, BUILDING COST MANUALS AND DATA COLLECTION SOURCES

COST MANUELS

Architectural Design Cost and Data, Pasadena, California, monthly.

Boeckh Building Valuation Manual, Milwaukee: American Appraisal Co., annually.

Building Construction Cost Data, Duxbury, Mass.: Robert Snow Means Co., annually.

Design Cost & Data, Glendora, California: Allan Thompson Publishers, bimonthly.

Dodge Building Cost Calculator and Valuation Guide, New York: McGraw-Hill Information Systems Co., quarterly.

Marshall Valuation Service, Los Angeles: Marshall and Swift Publication Co., monthly.

Real Estate Valuation Guide, Milwaukee: Boeckh Publications, monthly.

Residential Cost Handbook, Los Angeles: Marshall and Swift Publication Co., quarterly.

TRW-Redi Data, 1800 Northwest 66th Ave., Plantation, Florida 33313, property and tax data in print, and microfiche, in some states computerized with weekly updates.

Property Tax Consulting As A Business

A business that can be run by anyone from home, the property tax consultant business is extremely profitable. Finding customers is never a problem. Some earn over 6 figures yearly. Visit: http://propertytaxconsult.com for the full story. Sign up for the newsletter at http://propertytaxconsultingbusiness.com

ONLINE RESOURCES

Latest news from http://www.Realtor.org visit http://www.realtor.org

For yearly regional cost figures from **Remodeling Magazine Cost vs. Value Report From Remodeling Magazine** http://www.remodeling.hw.net

Online Appraisal Data

Most appraisers keep their ways of generating sales data information under tight wraps. Real Estate Appraisers can charge up to $500 for a Market Valuation Report for a home.

You can get detailed maps, lot sizes, square footage data, real time information inexpensively. However, this is just overview information. You still must take photos of your comparables and get detailed information which is best obtained from an actual visit to a real estate broker and getting "sold" MLS data.

[Option A] Personalized Home Valuation Report Price: $29.95
· Automated Valuation Model (AVM)
· Accurate Market Value
· Up to 15 Recent Comparable Sales

- Detailed Maps with Comps
- Real-Time Property Information
- Tax Assessor Data
- Lot Size, Square Footage
- Legal Description
- Sales History
- Charted Valuation - Trend Graphs

[Option B] Subject Property with Recent Sales Report Cost Price: $9.90
- Detailed Property Information
- Comparable Sales List
- Complete Tax Assessor Data
- Transaction History

Check Out Instant On-Line Appraiser!
http://www.electronicappraiser.com/uh.cfm?partnerID=292218

Note: You need to do a drive by to verify condition and pick out any additional or missing variables not addressed in the property report.

How To Make A Quick Rough Sketch For A Property Using Free Software

When you do have a case and need to work up a drawing for a more formal presentation for square footage, use this free resource. There's no learning curve, and you'll get professional results in just a few minutes, guaranteed.

http://www.smartdraw.com/specials/floorplans.asp?id=42023

Instantly create perfect floor plans in minutes. Includes thousands of ready-made graphics that you simply stamp to create your drawing. It's fast and easy and designs just about anything: House Plans, Landscapes, Decks, Kitchens, Bathrooms, Office Spaces, Facilities and more

MOBILE HOME COST GUIDES

N.A.D.A. Appraisal Guide, P.O. Box 7800, Costa Mesa CA, 92628, annual, 3 upgrades/yr.

Kelley Blue Book, 5 Oldfield Dr., Irvine, CA. 92714, annual, 2 upgrades/yr.

Mobile/Manufactured Home Blue Book, 29 North Wacker, Chicago, IL, 60606, annual, 2 upgrades/yr.

APPENDIX A: GLOSSARY

"Wisdom outweighs any wealth." - Sophocles

Abatement: A reduction or decrease in property taxes, approved by the taxing authority, initiated at the request of the taxpayer.

Acre: A unit of land of any shape that measures 43,560 square feet.

Adjustments: A decrease or increase in the sales price of a comparable property to account for a feature that the property has, or does not have, in comparison to the subject property.(92)

Ad Valorem Tax: Literally, Latin for "at value". A tax based on a fixed percentage of the property's value. The value of the property is determined by the tax assessor.

Annual Assessment Date: All comparable sales used for your property tax reduction must precede this date. Twelve months is acceptable, however, more recent comparables sales would be more favorable. A professional appraiser looks for data within 6 months of the date of sale and gives an explanation why any later comparable sales are used.

Appeal Process: The time requirements and specific process vary from state to state but have these features in common:

1. The appeal must be in writing and within a specific timeframe (before the annual assessment date). The appeal is typically made to the Tax Assessor but may only be to a Board of Appeals.
2. If satisfaction is not obtained from the local tax assessor, a second level of appeal can be made to the

County Board of Appeals (County Board of Equalization).
3. The last level of appeal is to the Tax Court level.

Apportion: Once the amount of taxes to be levied by each taxing district has been determined, the total tax levy must be divided, or apportioned, among all the taxation districts which contain territory in the jurisdiction.(93)

Appraisal: The act or process of estimating value.(94) Its estimate of probable selling price should be thorough, comprehensive, supportable and justifiable.

Appraised Value: An estimate of the fair market value of a particular property. This should be 100% of the property's market value.

Assessed Value: Value placed on land and buildings by a government tax assessor for use in levying property taxes. The assessed value of the property may be different than the appraised value.

Assessing Unit: The local government jurisdiction (county, city, town or village) having the responsibility for setting assessments.

Assessment Base: The assessed value of all property within a certain area, such as a tax district. Synonymous with the property tax base.

Assessment Change Notice: In some states this document is required when a property value is changed. Certain legal information will be required on this notice such as appeal instructions, change in current and previous year's value, appeal deadline date, etc.

Assessment District: See tax district.

Assessment Jurisdiction: The assessment jurisdiction is the county in which the subject property is located.

Assessment Roll: See tax roll.

Board of Equalization: A special group of state or county officials established for the purpose of adjusting inequitable tax assessments.

Class Ratio: The average percentage of market value that different classes of property are assessed at in a community; the classes consist of residential, apartment, commercial, etc.

Cost Estimating: The process of dividing a building into its components and estimating the value of each component. The estimated value of the building is the combination of these individual costs.

Current Ratio: See sales ratio.

Depreciation: "Depreciation is a loss in value from any cause. Deterioration, or physical depreciation, is evidenced by wear and tear, decay, dry rot, cracks, encrustation, or structural defects. Other types of depreciation are caused by obsolescence, either functional or external. Functional obsolescence may be caused by such items as inadequacy or superadequacy in size, style, or mechanical equipment. Physical deterioration and functional obsolescence are evident in the improvement. External obsolescence is caused by changes external to a subject property, such as changes in demand, changes in general property uses in the subject property's area, and changes in zoning, financing and national regulations."(95)

Director's Ratio: A range within the sales ratio that the market value must fall within for a taxpayer to qualify for a reduction in assessed valuation.

183

Easement: A right or privilege that one has in order to use land for a specific purpose. For example, a right of way for pipes, utility poles, private or public passage, etc.

Economic Life: An estimate of how long a structure will be used. When the structure contributes nothing to the value of the land, then the structure has ended its economic life.

Effective Age: The age that a structure appears to be when compared with other similar structures. The effective age is often different than the actual age because of differences in upkeep and maintenance, design or other economic considerations.

Estate: The degree of ownership a person has in real property.

Equalization Rate: A statistical average percentage of full value at which assessments were set by assessor(s) in an assessing unit. There is a lag between the valuation date on which an equalization rate is based and the year the rate is used. As a result, the equalization rate, in most cases, is unrelated to the current ratio between assessed value and market value that exists in a community.(96)

Equalized Full Value: Total assessed value of property divided by the equalization rate is the same as the equalized full value.

Exemption: A relief from the obligation of taxation on all or part of the assessed value of a property. An exemption may be awarded only on authorization of a specific state statute.

Expert Testimony: Testimony of a person or persons who are skilled in some art, science, profession or business, whose skill or knowledge is not common to others, and which has come to such experts by reason of special study and experience in such art, science, profession or business.(97)

Expert Witness: A person qualified to carry out expert testimony.

Farmland Assessment: Favorable tax treatment resulting in a lower assessment. Conditions vary from state to state, but it is generally the value of the land, not less than 5 acres, which is actively devoted to agricultural or horticultural use for at least 2 successive years preceding the tax year (annual assessment date).

Fee Simple: Sometimes called fee or fee simple absolute. It is the greatest possible estate or degree in the right of ownership and continues without time limitation.

Fractional Assessments: Any assessment made at less than current full value; the practice of assessing at less than full value.

Frontage: The length of the property's boundary that parallels the street. On a lakefront home, the frontage is the shore line.

Full Value: See market value.

Gross Living Area: Used by appraisers, it is the method for measuring the size of a house by measuring the outside of the house above the foundation. Each story is included. Areas such as basements, attics, porches or garages, are excluded from the total calculations.

Highest and Best Use: All land is appraised "as if vacant and available for its highest and best use." It is one of the most important principles in valuation and can have tremendous impact on the value of a property. The

185

highest and best use of the land must be legally and economically possible. It is the most profitable use of the land and must be physically possible.

Impact Notice: Following a general assessment or mass appraisal, a notice is sent to all property owners showing the old assessment and the impact of the new assessment.

Improvements: Improvements are buildings, additions to buildings, parking lots, decks, sidewalks, wells and/or other permanently attached additions to land.

Intangible Personal Property: This includes such things as stocks, bonds, notes and patents.

Leasehold: The right to possess and use real estate for a specific time created by a lease.

Level of Assessment: See sales ratio.

Location: An economic concept unique to real estate because of its immobility.

Lot and Block System: A legal description used in describing a parcel of land as found in the plat record of sub-dividable land.

Matched Pairs Extraction: The most accurate method to arrive at the value of an adjustment is to use matched pairs. Find sales of nearly identical properties with the item for which you are trying to determine the value. Compare sales of equally identical properties without that item. After adjusting for minor differences between the properties, their difference is the adjustment.

Market Value: The most probable price that a property will sell for in a free market of buyers and sellers, free from constraining pressures or unusual situations.

Mass Appraising: This is the process of valuing an entire area of properties at a given date, in a uniform order, using standard methodology, common reference for data, and allowing for statistical testing.

Mill: This equals one tenth of a cent. It is given as a percentage figure that everyone pays on the assessed value of their property. See tax rate.

Millage Rate: This is also known as the tax rate and is set by the county government. The millage rate is derived at by dividing the county's operating budget by the total assessed value in the county. A millage rate of 35 mills, or $35.00 per thousand, means that the assessed value of the property is multiplied by $35.00 for each thousand dollars of the assessment. See tax rate.

Multiple Listing Service (MLS): An association of real estate brokers that agrees to work together, pooling their data and cooperating to sell the group's listings.

Multiple Regression Analysis: A statistical approach to data collection using multiple observations, establishing essential parameters, identifying independent variables, and the dependent variable. Statistical reliability is projected giving a percentage of error confidence level.

Neighborhood: A separately identifiable area within a community retaining some quality or character which distinguishes it from other areas.

Notification Date: Date when new assessments become available to the public.

Obsolescence: One of the causes of depreciation brought about by changes in design, new concepts and/or new inventions.

187

Personal Property: Non-real items and tangible items not permanently attached to the ground. Permanent items would cause injury to the item or to the real estate if they were extracted.

PIN Number: Parcel identification number refers to block and lot number. Numbering system that identifies a property on a tax map, on the tax rolls and on your tax bill.

Plat: A plan, map or chart of a city, town or section, usually on land that has been subdivided, indicating boundaries and borders of individual properties. Each lot is identified by number and letter and lot dimensions are noted. It may also include features such as building locations, water pipes, sewer lines, vegetation, topography, etc.

Productive Use Value: Productive use value is that value which land has for agricultural and/or horticultural use.

Proper Filing Date: This is the date by which a formal appeal must be submitted to the taxing authorities. It may be "within 30 days from the date on the tax appraisal notice."

Property Classification: For property tax purposes, property is divided into three classes: (1) real property (2) tangible personal property and (3) intangible personal property. Real property is further sub-classified as: (1) residential, (2) agricultural/horticultural, and (3) utility, industrial, commercial railroad, etc.

Property Record Card: This card is found at the tax assessor's office and contains the information gathered on a particular property along with calculations used to determine assessed value.

Property Return Card: In some jurisdictions you may be required to file a property return card to receive eligible exemptions, to insure the tax bill is mailed to the correct address, or to trigger a change on the property value. In some jurisdictions, this "change notice" is the legal vehicle that formally permits the taxpayer to protest the taxes.

Property Tax Base: See assessment base.

Real Estate: This is the land itself and all things permanently attached to it.

Real Property: Real property refers to the rights of ownership of real estate.

Repairs: This is the expenditure for general upkeep to maintain the property close to the original condition. It does not include the renovation or replacement of any substantial part of the house.

Replacement Costs: This is the cost of construction to replace a similar building at current prices using up-to-date materials and a design meeting current building codes.

Residential Assessment Ratio (RAR): See sales ratio.

Revaluation: This is the mass appraisal of all property within an assessment district, municipality, county, parish, precinct, township, or ward to obtain equalization of assessed values.

Right of Way: The privilege to cross over the land of another by one person or persons. An easement.

Sales Ratio: Also may be called the average ratio, director's ratio, assessment level, the common level of 100% of true value, average percentage of full value, just valuation, the equalization rate (which may or may not be equivalent to the sales ratio in different states), RAR (residential assessment ratio), etc. The tax director has a legal directive to come up with this figure each year. He does this by tabulating all the assessed values on his tax rolls and collecting data from real estate market transactions in his area.

Site: A plot of land that has been improved or is suitable upon which to build.

Special Assessments: A variety of the property tax that requires that the rate of assessment must be uniform for all property within a particular special benefit classification.

Straight Line Depreciation: Depreciation method for tax purposes using equal amounts each year over the life of an asset.

Survey Method: When the number of comparable sales is limited in the market area, the appraiser may be unable to complete a matched pair extraction for value differences. In such cases, *cost data* for items such as area, air conditioning, storage, fireplace, etc., may be used. Survey results may be used to estimate value differences for features such as location, site or view, design and appeal, etc., because of the appraiser's inability to objectively measure value of these type features.(98)

Square Foot Cost: Dividing the market value or cost of construction by gross floor area in order to determine replacement, construction or reproduction cost of a building on a square foot basis.

Substitution: The principle of substitution says that the maximum value of a property tends to be set by the cost of an equivalent, equally desirable, similar substitute property at a certain date. The cost of an addition or the cost of remodeling work may not increase the value of your house by a value equivalent to the construction cost. The value of a component part of the property's value depends on the amount that it contributes to the value of the whole property. For example, if the cost of building an attached greenhouse is $16,000, the actual amount that it increases and contributes to the total property value may be only $3,000. A prudent buyer will buy a feature at the lowest price given a choice of features.

Tangible Personal Property: Includes such things as automobiles, boats, planes, farm implements which are moveable and are not attached to the land.

Tax Abatement: A decrease in the amount of property tax resulting in a refund of taxes due to the taxpayer.

Tax Base: The sum of all assessed property values in a community.

Taxing District: The specific area, such as a county, over which a taxing authority can levy taxes. Synonymous with assessment district.

Tax Due Date: Date by which you have to pay taxes. You still have to pay your taxes on time when appealing your taxes.

Tax Map: A map that shows by block and lot the boundaries of individual lots within a taxing district.

Tax Rate: The ratio of dollars of tax found by dividing the budget (the amount of money the local government will spend in one year) by the total assessed value of real estate in the taxing district. The tax rate is shown as dollars per hundred ($7.00 per hundred shown as .07) and may also be known as the mill rate (millage means per thousand. A millage rate quoted as 70 mills would be equivalent to a tax rate of $70.00 per thousand in valuation). Budget / Total Tax Base = Tax Rate

Example: Total tax base (total assessment of taxable property in the district) = $77,810,341

Total budget (bond debt, teachers, police and local government workers' salaries and expenses) = $1,271,133.

$1,271,133 / $77,810,341 =.0163 Tax Rate

.0163% = 16.3 mills (mills = 10ths of a cent per dollar assessment)

Tax Roll: The list of every taxpayer subject to property taxes within a taxing district, containing a description of the taxed parcels, assessed value and tax rate.

Tax Sale: The sale of property for unpaid taxes done by public auction.

Tax Year: The fiscal year may be different than the calendar year. Be sure that the tax appeal evidence is appropriate for the tax year appealed.

True Value: See market value.

Uniform Percentage of Value: See sales ratio.

Zoning: The division of a community into separate areas showing how the property in each zone may be developed such as residential, multi-family, local business district, light industrial, commercial park district, etc.

Endnotes

Attributions and source information

Chapter 2

[1] The Federal National Mortgage Association (FNMA), Section 410.01 Fannie Mae (FNMA) is the largest purchaser of single family home mortgages. Mortgage purchases are made from approximately 3,000 approved mortgage lenders throughout the country. These lenders then can obtain new funds and make new loans. Fannie Mae is the industry leader for standardizing form guidelines and establishing standards for appraisal practices by which homes are valued.

[2] Ventolo & Williams, *Fundamentals of Real Estate Appraisal, 5th Ed.,* Dearborn Financial Publishing, 1990, p. 288.

[3] The Federal National Mortgage Association (FNMA), Section 402.02.

[4] Shenkel, William M., *Real Estate Appraisal*, South-Western Publishing Co., 1992, p. 478.

[5] Fannie Mae Guidelines, Section 408.02, *Sales Comparison Analysis.*

[6] Rattermann, Mark, MAI, SRA, Consistency Problems in Residential Appraisals, *The Appraisal Journal , Oct. 1994, p. 518*

[7] *Single Family Residential Appraisal Manual*, Basis for estimating dollar adjustments, Farmers Home Loan Instructions 1922-C, 1993, p. 12.

[8] Adapted from 2005 - 2006 Cost vs. Value Report, *Remodeling Magazine*, December 2005. Online at http://www.realtor.org/rmomag.NSF/pages/feature1dec05?OpenDocument

[9] Opsata, Margaret, Renovation: What's it Worth, *Metropolitan Home*, 1993, p. 28. Reprinted with permission from the Metropolitan Home Magazine.

[10] *What Buyers Want,* National Association of Home Builders, 1989.

Chapter 3

[11] Federal National Mortgage Association (Fannie Mae) Customer Education Group, *The Appraisal Guide* Washington, D.C.: Fannie Mae, 1992, p. 28.

[12] Rhodes, Maxwell, MAI, *How to Appraise Your Own Home*, Delphi Books, 1980, p 32.

[13] Holland, Sherman T. and Robbin R. Hough, "Nuclear Power Plants and the Value of Agricultural Land," *Land Economics,* Feb. 1991, p. 30.

[14] *The URAR Uniform Residential Appraisal Report Handbook*, Fannie Mae-Section 404.01 (Location), National Association of Real Estate Appraisers, 1989, p. 8.

[15] *Property Assessment Valuation*, International Association of Assessing Officers, Chicago, 1977, p. 88.

[16] Stewart, James , QC, *Real Estate Appraisal in a Nutshell*, University of Toronto Press, 1972, p. 93.

[17] HUD Form 54891, HUD Handbook 4150.1 and 4145.1, U.S. Department of Housing & Urban Development, 6/85, p. 48.

[18] HUD Form 54891, HUD Handbook 4150.1 and 4145.1, U.S. Department of Housing & Urban Development, 6/85, p. 48-49.

[19] Rhodes, Richard Maxwell., *How to Appraise Your Own Home*, Delphi Books, 1980, p. 31.

[20] Miller and Gilbeau, *Residential Real Estate Appraisal*, Prentice-Hall, Inc., 1980, p. 38.

[21] Rinehart, James R., PhD, and Jeffrey J. Pompe, Ph.D., "Adjusting the Market Value of Coastal Property for Beach Quality," *The Appraisal Journal*, Oct. 1994, p. 604-608.

[22] *Fannie Mae Appraisal Guidelines,* Section 403.06.

[23] HUD Form 54891, HUD Handbook 4150.1 and 4145.1, U.S. Department of Housing & Urban Development, 6/85, p. 49.

[24] Seligman, Daniel, Ask Mr. Statistics, (earthquake predictions and property values), *Fortune,* Jan. 11, 1993, p. 104.

[25] Chalmers, James A., Ph.D., and Thomas O. Jackson, MAI, "Risk Factors in the Appraisal of Contaminated Property," *Appraisal Journal*, Jan. 1996, p. 58.

[26] *Associated Press,* July 28, 1994.

[27] Gay, Kathlyn, Franklin Watts, *Silent Killers: Radon and other Hazards,* 1988, p. 77.

[28] *Focus-The Bulletin of Environmental Risk Evaluation and Management,* Columbus, Ohio: Hazardous Materials Institute, March 30, 1990, p. 6.

[29] Josef, Hebert, H, "Tap water poses risk to millions, groups say," *Associated Press*, October 27, 1995.

[30] Nelson, J. Genereux and M. Genereux, *Land Economics,* Nov. 1992, p. 359.

[31] "Infinity Inc,." *Strategic Investments*, Financial Promotions Inc., March 1994, p. 2.

[32] "Fertilizer Nitrates in Rural Water Threaten Infants," *Associated Press,* 2/23/96.

[33] A Home Buyer's Guide to Environmental Hazards, publication of The U.S. General Services Administration, p. 27.

[34] Brilliant, Philip, "One-On-One: Dealing with Underground Storage Tanks-Part 2," *New Jersey Realtor®*, April 1994, p. 4.

[35] Bass, Sandra , et al. v. The Tax Commission of the City of New York, et al., N.Y. Sup. Ct. App. Div. 1992.

[36] "A Home Buyer's Guide to Environmental Hazards," a publication of the U.S. General Services Administration, p. 22.

[37] Redhead, Stephen and Christopher H. Dodge, *Health Effects of Power-Line Electromagnetic Fields*, Congressional Research Service, Library of Congress, 12/1/92, p. 8.

[38] Wertheimer, N. and E. Leeper. "Electrical Wiring Configurations and Childhood Cancer." *American Journal of Epidemiology,* 109, 1979, p. 273-284.

[39] Savitz, D.A., "Case-Control Study of Childhood Cancer and Exposure to 60-Hz Magnetic Fields." *American Journal of Epidemiology,* 128, 1988, p. 10-20.

[40] Tomenius, L. "50-hz Electromagnetic Environment and the Incidence of Childhood Cancers in Stockholm County." *Bioelectromagnetics*, 7/1986, p. 191-207.

[41] Sugarman, Ellen, *Warning: The Electricity Around You May Be Hazardous to Your Health*, Simon & Schuster, 1992, p. 107, p. 145.

[42] Criscuola v. Power Authority of the State of New York, 188 AD2d 951, 592 NYS2d 79 (3d Dept., 1992)

[43] Willsey v. Kansas City Power, 631 P2d 268, 277-278.

[44] Rikon, Michael, "Electromagnetic Radiation Field Property Devaluation," *The Appraisal Journal*, Jan. 1996, p. 88.

[45] Nazaroff, William and Anthony Nero, Jr., *Radon and Its Decay Products in Indoor Air*, John Wiley & Sons, 1988.

[46] Brenner, David, *Radon, Risk and Remedy*, W.H. Freeman and Co., NY, 1989, p. 102.

[47] *Investment Business Daily*, 2/23/98.

[48] EPA Radon Risk Evaluation Chart.

[49] *Evaluation of Occupational and Environmental Exposures to Radon and Radon Daughters in The United States*, NCRP Report No. 78, National Council on Radiation Protection and Measurements, 1985, p. 15.

[50] Pearson, J.E., "Natural Environmental Radioactivity from Radon-222," *U.S. Public Health Service Report 999-RH-26*, Public Health Service, Washington, D.C., 1967.

[51] Nelson, Jon P., "Airports and Property Values: A Survey of Recent Evidence," *Journal of Transport Economics and Policy*, January 1980.

[52] Frankel, "Aircraft Noise and Residential Property Values: Results of a Survey Study," *The Appraisal Journal,* Jan. 1991, p. 107.

[53] HUD Form 54891, HUD Handbook 4150.1 and 4145.1, Section 1.7, U.S. Department of Housing & Urban Development, 6/85, p. 49.

[54] Handbook 4905.1 Rev-1, Requirements for Existing Housing, U.S. Department of Housing & Urban Development, August 1991, p. 18.

[55] Hughes and Sirmans, "Traffic Externalities and Single-Family House Prices," *Journal of Regional Science,* Nov. 1992, p. 487.

[56] "Air Pollution 'Deadly Threat' to 23 Million," *Associated Press,* April 30, 1994.

[57] Rodriguez, Ph.D.., Mauricio, and C.F. Sirmans, SRPA, Ph.D., "Quantifying the Value of a View in Single-Family Housing Markets," *The Appraisal Journal,* Oct. 1994, p. 600-603.

[58] *The Appraisal of Real Estate,* 8th Ed., American Institute of Real Estate Appraisers, 1985, p. 39.

[50] Ludy, Andrew, *Condominium Ownership, a Buyer's Guide,* The Landing Press, 1982, p. 8.

[60] Adapted from "Quality of Construction," *Single Family Residential Appraisal Manual,* Farmers Home Loan Instructions 1922-C, 1993, p. 18.

[61] Rhodes, Richard Maxwell, M.A.I., *How To Appraise Your Own Home,* Delphi Books, 1980, p. 25.\

[62] Ibid. p. 27.

[63] Handbook 4905.1 Rev-1, "Requirements for Existing Housing," U.S. Department of Housing & Urban Development, August 1991, p. 21.

[64] Handbook 4905.1 Rev-1, "Requirements for Existing Housing," U.S. Department of Housing & Urban Development, August 1991, p. 21

[65] Ibid., p. 13.

[66] Ibid., p. 13.

[67] Schnolsky, Rick, "EIFS." *Builder*, Mar. 1996, p. 168.

[68] Seldin, Maury, *The Real Estate Handbook*, from the chapter "Value Analysis: The Market Comparison Approach," by Donald McCandless, Dow Jones-Irwin, 1980.

[69] Adapted from: "Room List," U. S. Dept. of Housing and Urban Development Handbook 4150.1, Revision 2, Chapter 8, 1993.

[70] Williams and Ventolo, *How To Use the Uniform Residential Appraisal Report*, Dearborn Financial Publishers, 1991, p. 150.

[71] Adapted from, "Above Grade Room Count-Gross Living Area (Size)," *Single Family Residential Appraisal Manual*, Farmers Home Loan Instructions 1922-C, 1989, p. 20.

[72] Rhodes, Richard Maxwell, M.A.I., *How To Appraise Your Own Home* , Delphi Books, 1980, p. 26.

[73] *The Uniform Residential Appraisal Report Handbook* by Fannie Mae, compiled by National Association of Real Estate Appraisers, Scottsdale, AZ, Section 406.05, 1989, p. 70.

[74] "Energy-Efficient Properties," Fannie Mae, section 305.01.

[75] Adapted from "Special Energy Efficient Items," *Single Family Residential Appraisal Manual*, Farmers Home Loan Instructions 1922-C, 1989, p. 26.

[76] Mills, Arlen C., MAI, Adapted from, "The Uniform Residential Appraisal Report," American Institute of Real Estate Appraisers, 1988, p. 51.

[77] "Fannie Mae Appraisal and Review Appraisal Guidelines," National Association of Real Estate Appraisers, 1992, p. 31.

[78] "Sales Comparisons Analysis-Age," *U.S. Dept. of Housing and Urban Development Handbook*

Chapter 4

[79]*Property Assessment Valuation* by International Association of Assessing Officers, 1977, p. 136.

Chapter 5

[80] Farmers Home Administration (FmHA Instructions 1922-C-Subpart C) portion that applies to : "The appraisal of single family residential properties," 1/27/93, p. 17.

Chapter 6

[81] Smith and Lohse, "Slashing the taxes on your home," *Money*, Jan 1993, p. 96.

[82] Dotzour, Mark G., "An Empirical Analysis of the Reliability and Precision of the Cost Approach in Residential Appraisal," *Journal of Real Estate Research*, (Summer 1990).

[83] Dotzour, Mark G., SRA, Ph.D. and Mark Freitag, SRA, "The Cost Approach in Residential Appraising," *The Appraisal Journal*, April 1995, p. 185.

[84] "1991 County, City and Town Assessment Rolls," *Exemptions From Real Property Taxation In New York*, New York, 1993, p. 3.

Chapter 7

[85] Carroll, E. Jean, "Ask E. Jean," contributing editor to *Esquire* and television hostess.

[86] Elias Stephen, Mary Randolph, Barbara Kate Repa, Ralph Warner, *Legal Breakdown*, NOLO Press, 1991, p.70.

Chapter 9

[87] *The Appraisal of Real Estate*, 6th edition, American Institute of Real Estate Appraisers, 1973, p. 242.

[88] Carnahan, Dollar & Steele, *Principles of Residential Real Estate Appraising*, National Association of Independent Fee Appraisers, Inc., 6/81, p. 31.

Chapter 10

[89] Excerpts from "Buyer Beware""" to "Broker Take Care"-*A Realtor®'s Guide to Avoiding Liability for Undisclosed Property Defects*, Legal Liability Series, Copyright, 1988, NATIONAL ASSOCIATION OF REALTORS®. Reprinted with permission.

[90] Adapted from, "New Disclosure Laws for Home Sellers," by Hal Portor, *Mechanix*, March 1994, p. 28 and Realtors Web-site http://www.tmgrp.com/tmg/sccar/library/prp_disc.html

[92] This list is adapted from: *The Price Waterhouse Personal Tax Advisor*, 1994-1995 Special Edition, Price Waterhouse, 1994, p.128-130.

Glossary

[92] Williams and Ventolo, *How To Use the Uniform Residential Appraisal Report*, Dearborn Financial Publishers, 1991, p. 8.

[93] *Guide for the Property Owner*, Wisconsin Department of Revenue, 1993, p. 1.

[94] *Uniform Standards of Professional Appraisal Practice*, Jan. 1, 1989.

[95] Reprinted with permission from The Appraisal of Real Estate, Tenth Edition, © 1992, p. 343, by the Appraisal Institute, Chicago, IL.

Made in the USA
Lexington, KY
20 March 2013